Jackson's Valley Campaign
The Battle Of McDowell
March 11 - May 18, 1862

2nd Edition

Richard L. Armstrong

Manufactured in the United States by
H. E. Howard, Inc., Lynchburg, Virginia

Printed by H. E. Howard, Inc.

ISBN-0-930919-98-X

Dedication

This book is dedicated to God, without Whose guidance it would not have been written. It is further dedicated to my grandfather, Robert Azariah Armstrong (1858-1936), who as a youngster listened to the echoing roar of the artillery at the Battle of McDowell.

ACKNOWLEDGEMENTS

Lasting gratitude is expressed to Harold E. Howard for undertaking the publication of **The Virginia Civil War Battles and Leaders Series.**

My thanks to Lt. Col. Robert J. Driver, Jr. for his suggestions and comments concerning this volume.

Thanks to Sharon I. Lindsay and Jeannette B. Robinson of the Bath County Cooperative Library for their patience and for processing innumerable inter-library loans.

Thanks also are due Raymond W. Watkins and Robert K. Krick for their contribution of materials in compiling this work.

Thanks to Lowell Reidenbaugh for his suggestions and contributions in making this volume something to be proud of. Thanks for your hard work.

I wish also to thank the owners of the McDowell battlefield for allowing Franklin Taylor and me to visit the area.

And finally, to all those who assisted in some manner on this volume, and are not mentioned above, I say thank you.

Richard L. Armstrong

TABLE OF CONTENTS

CHAPTER I

Operations To April 7, 1862

The small army of Brigadier General Edward "Alleghany" Johnson endured the winter hardships of 1861-1862 on top of Alleghany Mountain. The major portion of the command occupied the fortifications at that point, which was known as Camp Alleghany to the Confederates and as Camp Baldwin to the Federals. The remainder of Johnson's command was in the valley below, as well as other nearby locations. On December 13, 1861, Johnson had successfully repelled an attempt by Brigadier General Robert H. Milroy to drive him from his mountain stronghold. After the failure of that attempt, Milroy went into winter quarters until the middle of March, 1862.

On March 11, President Abraham Lincoln created a new military district, the Mountain Department. Major General John C. Fremont, better known as the "Pathfinder of the West", was assigned to it's command. At this time President Lincoln believed it was possible to march from Western Virginia over the mountains into Eastern Tennessee, and seize the railroad at Knoxville. General Fremont, realizing that it was an impractical idea, promised that with an adequate force, he would undertake the campaign.[1]

General Fremont requested additional troops for this purpose, and in response, the president ordered Brigadier General Louis Blenker's division to join Fremont. This reassignment removed 10,000 troops from the Army of the Potomac that Major General George B. McClellan was assembling at Yorktown for operations against Richmond, the capitol of the Confederacy.

On March 16, General Milroy, in command of the Cheat Mountain District, proposed a plan for a spring campaign to Brigadier General William S. Rosecrans. General Rosecrans at that time was in command of the Mountain Department. General Milroy wrote:

> My plan would be, with 3,000 infantry and good batteries, to march 7 miles beyond Cheat Top, and there take a new road, not altogether cut out, to Greenbank, which place is 8 miles to [the] left of [Camp] Baldwin. From Greenbank proceed to Huntersville, which is now occupied by a regiment of infantry, several hundred cavalry, and two pieces of artillery. There effect junction with such force as General Cox may send from Lewisburg, and on good pike march to [the] rear of Alleghany,

1

now occupied by [a] force of about 2,000, according to my best information. Thence march rapidly to Staunton, or, if thought best, on to [the] Virginia and Tennessee road.[2]

General Milroy's command at this time amounted to just over 6,000 men, scattered over a considerable area. It was comprised of the following infantry regiments (or portions thereof): 25th Ohio, 32nd Ohio, 73rd Ohio, 75th Ohio, 2nd (West) Virginia, 3rd (West) Virginia and 10th (West) Virginia. The 1st (West) Virginia Cavalry also was a part of this command, as well as Captain Rigby's Indiana Battery.[3]

On March 18, General Johnson reported the strength of his command to General Robert E. Lee, who was then in Richmond. Further, "Old Alleghany" reported the positions that this troops then occupied, as well as the political sentiments of the citizens of that area. He wrote:

The prospect of calling to my aid volunteers from the country in which I am operating is by no means flattering. The people of this country are many of them, if not disloyal, at least indifferent as to which cause triumphs, and are willing to range themselves on the stronger side. The population is sparse, the country very mountainous.[4]

In response, General Lee ordered Johnson to call out the militia in his area, in compliance with the proclamation of Governor John Letcher, and fill up his companies.

Johnson reported further that the major portion of his command was stationed at Camp Alleghany, which had been strengthened considerably since it was attacked by Federals in December and now included ten pieces of artillery. A small portion of Johnson's troops was stationed at Huntersville, in Pocahontas County (now West Virginia). General Johnson described the position as being "weak."[5] A third detachment of Johnson's command was at Crab Bottom (now Blue Grass), in Highland County. There was also a small cavalry force stationed at Franklin, (Pendleton County, West Virginia) with orders to scout in all directions and be alert for any movement of the enemy. In addition, there were several companies of cavalry at Monterey, and one company of Tennessee Cavalry (Captain D. W. Alexander) at Warm Springs.[6] The Bath Cavalry, along with a portion of the Tennessee Cavalry was at Bath Alum Springs, in Bath County.

The effective strength of the various units was as follows:

Huntersville	500 for duty
Crab Bottom	350 for duty
Franklin	40 for duty
Monterey	60 for duty

Camp Alleghany . . . . 1,834 for duty
Total . . . . 2,784 for duty

In addition to these figures, there were another 1,179 men, absent for various reasons, giving Johnson a total of nearly 4,000 men.[7]

General Johnson's command then consisted of the following infantry regiments: 12th Georgia, 25th, 31st, 44th, 52nd and 58th Virginia, as well as Hansbrough's 9th Virginia Battalion. Along with the above mentioned infantry regiments, Johnson had three batteries of artillery: Miller's (four guns), Raine's (four guns) and Rice's (four guns). Also on hand were Alexander's Tennessee Cavalry, the Charlotte Cavalry, the Churchville Cavalry, the Pittsylvania Cavalry (on furlough) and the Rockbridge Cavalry.[8]

The Bath Cavalry was omitted from the report by Adjutant Edward Willis. Very likely it was included with Captain Alexander's Company, as they operated together until April 16, when Captain Alexander returned to Tennessee.

In the same letter reporting his strength to General Lee, Johnson commented: "There is but one point beyond this toward Staunton which I regard as defensible — Shenandoah Mountain, 26 miles from Staunton and about 19 from Monterey."[9] On March 21, General Lee instructed Johnson to send a competent officer to Shenandoah Mountain to ascertain if it was defensible and offered the necessary accommodations for troops. General Lee added: "Should you ascertain that the Shenandoah [Mountain] affords the best position in your rear for defending the approaches to Staunton, and preparations can be made for its occupation by your troops without disclosing your views to the enemy, it will be well for you to do so."[10]

General Johnson's position at Camp Alleghany was described as: ". . . although regarded impregnable in itself yet such was its location that the enemy by marching troops from Moorefield in Hardy County, could compel its evacuation without a direct attack in front and by thus coming in the rear intercept supplies and cut off retreat."[11] This threat, coupled with General Jackson's maneuverings in the Shenandoah Valley, did indeed compel Johnson to abandon this strong position.

According to Captain S. G. Pryor of the 12th Georgia Infantry, Johnson's men were greatly excited over the prospect of a withdrawal from Camp Alleghany to Shenandoah Mountain. While the move was unconfirmed, Pryor said, "I believe it myself."[12]

The excitement over falling back was caused by the news that Jackson's army was falling back from Winchester. By March 22, however, the excitement had subsided. General Jackson had been reinforced in the Valley, and everyone felt more at ease. But the sense of security felt by

3

Johnson's men was soon to end.

The armies of General Jackson and General James Shields met in armed conflict on March 23, 1862, at Kernstown, a few miles south of Winchester. Outnumbered more than two to one, Jackson's men fought desperately for a little more than two hours. As night fell, the Federals disengaged themselves and silence fell over the dead and dying.

The day following the fight at Kernstown, Jackson started moving leisurely up the Valley. His rear was protected by the ever-vigilant cavalry of Colonel Turner Ashby and Captain R. P. Chew's battery of artillery.

By early April, most of the Valley Army was in camp at Rude's Hill, on the Valley Turnpike. A portion of Jackson's command was posted near Stony Creek, while Colonel Ashby's cavalry was at Stony Creek itself, about ten miles north of Rude's Hill. Other than some periodic skirmishing between Ashby's cavalry and the Federal advance, the situation in the Valley was at a standstill.

Meanwhile, the Confederate contingent at Huntersville was preparing to pull up stakes. The command was under Major Alexander Caldwell Jones, of the 44th Virginia Infantry. Major Jones had been detached from his regiment in the fall of 1861 and placed in command of a small force of infantry and cavalry. Major Jones informed General Johnson that his command would be ready to leave Huntersville on Monday, March 31.

At this same time, in compliance with instructions from General Lee, Johnson issued a call for the militia units in his area to report for duty. The response was discouraging. The reason was quite clear, reported Colonel J. H. Johnson, who commanded the 46th Virginia Militia in Pendleton County (now West Virginia). Writing to General Johnson, the colonel said, "The idea has obtained in my County [Pendleton] that you are about to leave your present position [Camp Alleghany] and that our County will be abandoned to the ravages of the enemy. Therefore many have refused to respond to the call."[13]

Despite difficulties in mustering the Pendleton County Militia, Colonel Johnson reported to General Johnson on the 28th with the few men that had responded to the call. That same day, the Highland County Militia reported for duty.

Again Johnson's camp grew excited about falling back. This time, however, orders had been issued to pack up the baggage, indicating that this was more than a mere rumor. Where were the troops going? Speculation had it that Johnson would join General Jackson's army near Harrisonburg. Captain Pryor, however, did not agree. He felt that it was hardly reasonable that this route to Staunton would be left unguarded, permitting the enemy to get behind them.[14]

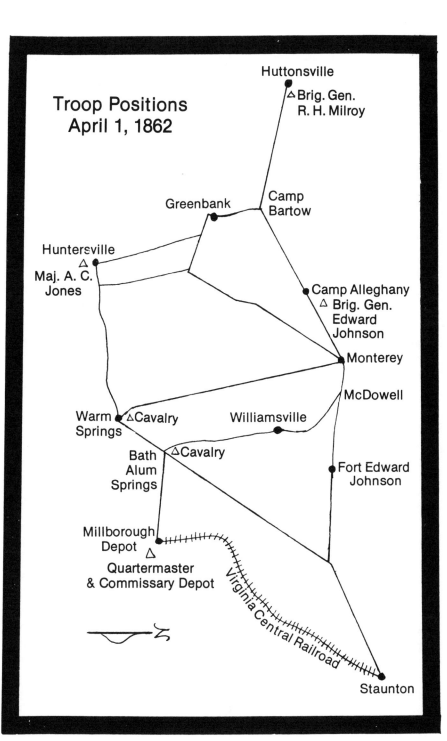

Troop Positions
April 1, 1862

Huttonsville
△ Brig. Gen.
R. H. Milroy

Greenbank

Camp
Bartow

Huntersville
△
Maj. A. C.
Jones

Camp Alleghany
△ Brig. Gen.
Edward
Johnson

Monterey

McDowell

Warm
Springs
△Cavalry

Williamsville

Bath
Alum
Springs
△Cavalry

Fort Edward
Johnson

Millborough
Depot
△
Quartermaster
& Commissary Depot

Virginia Central Railroad

Staunton

Three days later, the prospect of moving was now a reality. Between two and three hundred wagons had arrived at Camp Alleghany to pick up the baggage. At 4 a.m., on the morning of April 1, the sound of the drum aroused the men for the mornings work. By 8 a.m. the wagons were fully loaded and moving off for Shenandoah Mountain. To allow the wagons to reach the new camp, Johnson's army remained at their old camp with two days rations and a blanket apiece.[15]

General Johnson evacuated his camp on the top of Alleghany Mountain at 10 a.m. on April 2, falling back to Monterey. The abandonment of the camp saddened both the soldiers and the citizens alike. The soldiers felt they were abandoning their homes and loved ones. The citizens felt they were being left to the mercy of the heathen Yankees, who were sure to follow. At Monterey, the night being a cold one, the men sought shelter in barns, out buildings, churches, and the Court House. A number of the men were given shelter by the townspeople.

As General Johnson was leaving Camp Alleghany, the force at Huntersville, moved back to Warm Springs, in Bath County.

General Johnson resumed his march on April 3, leaving behind a company of cavalry from Rockbridge County. Later in the day, Johnson's command pitched their tents at McDowell, on the farm of Robert Sitlington, along the Bull Pasture River. While here, rumor reached General Johnson that the Federals were in pursuit of his army. Despite the rumor of danger, Johnson rested at McDowell until April 5.

On the same day that Johnson evacuated Camp Alleghany, military affairs escalated in the Lower Shenandoah Valley. General Banks, who had been in camp along Tom's Brook, at last took the initiative and moved across that stream. Almost at once he clashed with Colonel Ashby's cavalry, still acting as Jackson's rear guard. General Banks pressed on to Edinburg, a distance of ten miles, driving the cavalry before him.[16]

On the night of April 3, General Milroy was ordered to advance "cautiously", without artillery into the Valley of Virginia.[17] Earlier that same day, General Fremont complained to the War Department that the opportunity to capture Camp Baldwin [Camp Alleghany] had been lost due to the lack of horses to pull Milroy's artillery.

Before leaving Cheat Mountain, on April 5, General Milroy sent out several scouting parties. He ordered Captain George R. Latham to take eighty men from Companies B and K, 2nd (West) Virginia Infantry, and make a scout in the direction of Monterey. Another force, numbering some 300 men of the 25th Ohio Infantry under Colonel George Webster, was sent to Pendleton County, to guard against guerrillas operating in that area. If possible, Captain Latham was to form a junction with Colonel Webster, and move on Monterey. On the first night out this force camped at the foot of Alleghany Mountain. The following day, it passed through heavy timber to the summit of Alleghany Mountain. Then, moving by way of Circleville and Crab Bottom, it "quietly entered the town of Monterey."[18]

Apparently, Latham found no trace of Colonel Webster's command. These were the first Federal troops to enter the town, and they held it until the remainder of the regiment came up.

The cavalry left at Monterey by General Johnson had moved their camp to McDowell on the 5th. There they were joined by the Charlotte Cavalry, another cavalry company from Rockbridge County, and part of the Bath Cavalry.[19]

News of Captain Latham's occupation of Monterey with his small force quickly reached the Confederates on Shenandoah Mountain. Immediately, plans were made to send a force to Monterey in an attempt to capture Captain Latham's party.

About 11 p.m. on the night of April 6, the 12th Georgia Infantry was directed to prepare two days rations and be ready to march before morning. At the appointed time the Georgians formed up. As they started on their westward march, the men began to grumble about the direction they were going.

After marching about five miles, the column halted briefly, then resumed its trek. They reached McDowell about noon, where they again halted. While at McDowell, it commenced to snow and rain. Due to the weather, it was decided to delay marching any further until midnight. That way they would reach Monterey near daylight on April 8, and attack the Yankees then.

The scheme never materialized, however. About 9 p.m., an unidentified woman approached the camp with important information. She informed the Confederates that there were now some 2,000 Federal soldiers at Monterey. Consequently, the 12th Georgia returned to Fort Johnson on April 8.[20]

General Milroy left his camp on Cheat Mountain at 2 p.m. on April 5 and marched on the Greenbrier River. There he occupied the old Confederate position known as Camp Bartow. The following day, about 1 p.m., Milroy's command entered the fortifications on top of Alleghany Mountain, where they remained until the 7th. The camp here was described as "a dreary, dismal place."[21]

The unit's progress was reported to Edwin M. Stanton in Washington. In reply, the secretary of war informed Fremont that Blenker's division was en route to Harpers Ferry.

Orders were sent at once to General Milroy, instructing him to:

Occupy Monterey or some point west of it, where you can

maintain yourself against superior forces, and guard the road, concentrating at Monterey. General Schenck has been ordered to advance from Romney and Moorefield to operate on the road leading by Elkhorn to Franklin, in connection with the movement of General Banks up the valley of the Shenandoah.[22]

When Johnson moved from McDowell on April 5, he left behind a squadron (two companies) of cavalry, with instructions to complete their organization, perfect themselves in the drill, and scout the road leading toward the enemy. The summit of Shenandoah Mountain was gained that same morning. Once on the crest, Johnson began to construct fortifications. Captain S. G. Pryor, of the 12th Georgia, reported a week later that three regiments occupied the position on top of the mountain. He commented further that it was a very strong position and it would take an overwhelming force to drive them from it. The remainder of Johnson's command camped at the eastern base of Shenandoah Mountain, where there is a place known today as the "Georgia Flats" or "Georgia Camp."[23]

General Milroy, now aware that Latham was in possession of Monterey, ordered Colonel Moss to reinforce Latham with 400 men of the 2nd (West) Virginia Infantry. One soldier, writing of the march from Camp Alleghany to Monterey, said that it was "one of the roughest and most disagreeable marches we had yet experienced."[24] The cause of the discomfort was the snow that started falling late on the morning of the 6th. Melting rapidly, the snow turned the roadbed into a quagmire that severely impeded the progress of the Federals. General Milroy, who had planned to send the 75th Ohio and Hyman's Battery to Monterey on the 8th, further divided his command. He sent 300 men of the 32nd Ohio to Huntersville with orders to rejoin the command at Monterey. The general added:

> To-morrow [I] will scout [the] country in that vicinity and 10 miles down the Greenbrier with a company of cavalry. Will throw all the force I can into Monterey. We must have more transportation immediately; quartermaster's present supplies too limited to furnish us with subsistance. Think supplies can go to Monterey at half the cost and labor from New Creek via Franklin. I will move my headquarters to Monterey to-morrow. Terrible snow-storm here to-day.[25]

Here, for the first time, there is a hint of a problem that would plague Milroy throughout the campaign — the job of supplying his army.

In a letter to his wife, Milroy expressed growing concern for the safety of Colonel Webster and his men. He had received no word of them in five days and said he hoped to find them when he arrived in Monterey. The general also wrote that "I am pushing on as fast as Fremont will let me."[26]

At that time, April 6, Milroy felt that Fremont would hold him at Monterey, until General Robert Schenck's command arrived at Franklin. Milroy was then under the mistaken impression that Schenck was marching from Moorefield to Franklin.

In reality, Fremont telegraphed Schenck on April 7, with instructions not to "move beyond Moorefield until further orders."[27] General Schenck, still at Cumberland, Maryland, informed Fremont that he would start for Moorefield as soon as possible.

CHAPTER II

April 8 to 13, 1862

General Robert Milroy and his command left Camp Alleghany at 10 a.m. on April 8, 1862. Three hours later they arrived at Monterey,[1] where they discovered that a number of citizens had fled the town on the heels of the reatreating Confederates. The empty houses were utilized immediately as quarters for the Federal troops.

Shortly after the occupation of Monterey, a scouting party of the 2nd (West) Virginia Infantry was sent into the surrounding hills. A Rebel force was encountered and a few shots were exchanged, but without noticeable damage to either party. That night, Yankee pickets skirmished with the enemy, again with no harm to either side.

The following incident, recorded by William T. Price, very likely took place at this time. According to Price, a young Presbyterian Minister, a detachment of cavalry left McDowell, scouting toward Monterey. When near Monterey, the Confederates observed a group of armed men approaching under a flag of truce. It was soon discovered that this group of men were Federal troops, who had mistaken the Confederate cavalrymen for a group of citizens and had taken this precaution in approaching them.

When the two parties had drawn closer together, the Federals halted and issued the challenge: "Who comes there?" Before any answer could be made, the Unionists discovered they were in the presence of Confederate cavalry. Immediately taunts and insults were shouted at the horsemen, an action, wrote Price, that "was spiritedly resented."[2]

Sheltered by the flag of truce, the Yankees prepared to fire upon the cavalrymen. When their intentions became clear to the Confederates, they quickly turned their horses and fled. Although the Federals fired a number of shots at them, there were no injuries reported.[3]

After this incident, the Confederate pickets were strengthened in the direction of Monterey. During the following week there were several brushes between the two armies. The Confederates reported no losses during this period while General Milroy reported only a few men slightly wounded.[4]

On April 9, General Milroy informed Fremont that blinding snow storms, freezing rain and high water prevented him from bringing up supplies from the rear. He stated further that he had learned from refugees that there was an abundance of supplies in the Shenandoah Valley. "I think we should hasten there as speedily as possible," he concluded.[5]

In addition to his complaints about the inclement weather, Milroy reported the position of the Confederates in his front. General Johnson's brigade was on top of Shenandoah Mountain, 21 miles distant. Furthermore, a cavalry force, numbering about 300, was at McDowell, 10 miles distant. General Milroy informed his superior, that ". . . as soon as [the] weather permits, if they remain there, I will bag them."[6]

Plagued as he was with problems of supply, General Milroy encouraged his men to forage throughout the countryside. Frank S. Reader, a member of the 2nd (West) Virginia Infantry, remembered:

> Here the true act of foraging, in all its varied aspects, was learned by the boys, and they were apt pupils. For the first time we were in the enemy's country where there was something to eat, and other duties kept the officers and guards from scrutinizing too closely the mysterious movements of some of the men, who seemed to be unusually active in the service of their country. The farmers in the neighborhood could explain everything but they did not, and meanwhile the soldiers lived on the best that the country afforded.[7]

General Milroy's growing concern over the missing detachment of the 25th Ohio came to an end on April 9 when Colonel Webster arrived at Monterey with his command intact. Two days later, Milroy's command was reinforced by the arrival of the 75th Ohio Infantry at Monterey.

Meanwhile at McDowell, Confederate cavalry were placed on alert by a report that a strong enemy force was advancing on the village. Wagons were hitched and loaded and the troopers ordered to be ready to move at a moment's notice. Captain John R. McNutt of the 2nd Rockbridge Dragoons was sent into the mountains to scout out the enemy's position, and if possible to form an ambuscade. The Churchville Cavalry and a detachment of the Bath Cavalry were held in reserve, ready to go to McNutt's assistance if he should be overpowered. When Captain McNutt discovered that the report of Federal forces in the vicinity was unfounded, the cavalry was ordered about 9 p.m. to return to their quarters. However, as a precaution against a surprise attack, the wagons were left loaded and the horses saddled.[8]

On the night of the 10th, Companies C, F and H of the 2nd (West) Virginia Infantry and a small cavalry contingent left Monterey on a scout toward McDowell. In the early morning hours of April 11, at a bridge about six miles west of McDowell, they encountered a small force of Confederate cavalry. The Yankees charged and drove the Rebels back into their camp, during which action the Federals "were treated to a lively return of bullets." Two of the Yankee cavalrymen and one infantryman (of

11

Company F) were wounded.[9]

Fearing that the Federals were advancing in force on their position, the Confederate commander deemed it advisable to fall back to Shaw's Ridge, seven miles to the east. The withdrawal commenced just after sunrise, and after going a few miles, they were met by General Johnson, who ordered them back to McDowell. Reverend Price stated that the general "gave them a good cussing," and directed them to post strong pickets near the mountain to the west.[10]

While all this was taking place, General Fremont informed the War Department that he wished to reinforce General Milroy, but was uncertain of what troops were at his disposal. The secretary of war replied that all troops in the department, with the exception of those under General G. W. Morgan, were available to him. General Fremont was assured by the secretary that Louis Blenker's division, supposedly in the vicinity of Winchester, would be sent forward as quickly as possible.

On the same day, April 11, General Milroy advised Fremont that the Greenbrier River was swollen past the fording stage. As a result, supply trains were held up. Furthermore, the condition of the roads prevented General Robert Schenck, who was in dire need of supplies himself, from assisting Milroy from the direction of Moorefield.[11]

The day after their "dressing down" by General Johnson, the Confederate scouts performed their duties with a greater degree of efficiency. Leaving their horses at a convenient point and crossing the mountain on foot, the scouts advanced to within sight of Monterey. In the town, they saw ten tents, seven wagons and about 15 men. Assuming from this that only a very small force occupied Monterey at that time, they hurried to report this to General Johnson.[12]

The general was appalled. Could such a small enemy force induce so much fear in his cavalry? Before leaving Shenandoah Mountain, Johnson had ordered the 52nd Virginia to follow him. With that regiment, he planned to reconnoiter the enemy's strength and position. Based on the dispatches he had received, Johnson concluded that the force in his front was too powerful for his cavalry. He also needed to know if the enemy was advancing on the Staunton-Parkersburg Turnpike or moving south toward Warm Springs.

When his scouts reported the meager force in his front, Johnson was amused. He snickered at the prospect of 1,000 infantry and 300 cavalry attacking a handful of Yankees. Still, because many of the men were new to the service, "Old Alleghany" felt they could use the experience.

When the 52nd Virginia arrived at McDowell in the early evening, they were at once informed of the orders for them to march at 1 a.m. on April 12. During the hours that followed, however, Dr. David B. Lang, a highly efficient scout, reported that the Yankees had been reinforced and were preparing to receive an attack. In view of this latest intelligence, Johnson countermanded his earlier order. Instead of the 1 o'clock marching order, the troops were directed to set out just after daylight. General Johnson also sent for two pieces of artillery to come up from Fort Johnson, on Shenandoah Mountain.[13]

On April 12, Blenker's division was reported between Manassas Junction and Front Royal. The division, now commanded by General W. S. Rosecrans, was ordered to proceed to Moorefield, in Hardy County.

As Blenker's division meandered westward, General Milroy fired off a new salvo of complaints to Fremont. First of all, griped the peacetime lawyer from Rensselaer, Indiana, his army was reduced in strength by the numerous posts and stations that had to be manned in Western Virginia. None of his regiments, he said, was at full strength. ". . . if there is a live Governor at Wheeling," Milroy wrote, he should organize the home guards to relieve regular troops from this duty.[14] If this were done, and the men who were replaced were returned to his command, Milroy reported he would then have at least one full regiment.

General Milroy complained further about the lack of transportation facilities for his men, and added that there were two guns of Hyman's battery at Beverly that he could put to good use.

At about 8 a.m. on the morning of April 12, Johnson's column started for Monterey. The Confederates encountered Milroy's pickets about 9 o'clock on Jack Mountain, four miles east of Monterey, and drove them back approximately three hours later. When General Milroy learned that his pickets were under attack, he ordered eight companies — two each from the 75th Ohio, the 2nd (West) Virginia, the 32nd Ohio and the 25th Ohio — along with a company of cavalry and one gun from Hyman's battery to act as skirmishers.[15] Colonel Webster, who was placed in charge of the Union force, was ordered to meet the attack from behind rocks and trees and to fall back into the valley if he was badly outnumbered.

Colonel Webster and his skirmishers disappeared up the mountain where the general expected them to be attacked at any moment and his main line of defense assaulted. It was Milroy's impression that Johnson was returning to Monterey with his full force, and would attempt to surround his position. To guard against such a move, Milroy formed his line of battle on either side of the town — the 2nd (West) Virginia, the 32nd Ohio and the 75th Ohio Regiments on the right, the 25th Ohio and a battery of artillery on the left.

The skirmishers contested the ground gallantly before they were compelled to retire. An hour after they vanished in the hills, the skirmishers reappeared on the brow of the mountain, where they were clearly visible from Monterey.

After the Confederates crossed Jack Mountain, Dr. Lang, in charge of the scouts, reported to Lieut. Colonel Michael G. Harman that the enemy, about 4,000 strong, was in line of battle and prepared to receive an attack. In addition, Lang reported that Federal artillery was stationed on a conical hill south of Monterey and would be able to fire on them as they advanced. This information was relayed to Johnson, who had remained at McDowell. Immediately he ordered Captain Miller to take two guns from his battery and cover Colonel Harman's retreat.

As soon as the Confederates were sighted, Captain Hyman's battery opened fire on them from Dinwiddie's Gap.[16] The fire was directed to a low spot in the mountain where the road was known to cross. Several shells came shrieking through the tree tops and fell near Harman's men, many of whom were green troops, who "dodged beautifully" according to their veteran comrades of eleven months service.[17]

When the Federal artillery opened fire, the Union skirmishers ceased fire, because the southerners fell back and, according to one participant, "stopped our amusement."[18] A Union cavalry company was sent in pursuit of the retreating Rebels. The horsemen overtook their quarry after a five mile chase and engaged in a rearguard skirmish for about a mile before encountering Captain Miller's two guns. This brought a quick end to the action. The Rebels fell back to Shaw's Fork, near their fortifications on Shenandoah Mountain.

General Milroy maintained his line of battle at Monterey for several hours, hopeful that the engagement would be resumed. When that failed to occur, Milroy engaged in a period of self-recrimination. He berated himself for not having thrown a stronger force against the enemy.

The loss to the Yankees consisted of two men killed and three wounded, two of whom belonged to the 75th Ohio. According to Federal accounts, several Confederates were seen to fall, but how many was undetermined because they were removed from the field by their comrades. In reality, no Southerner was wounded in the skirmish at Monterey. Inhabitants of the town informed Milroy that the Confederate force numbered 1,500 men, plus two pieces of artillery, led by Johnson himself. Exactly how this intelligence was obtained by the citizens was never explained.

General Fremont, learning of the day's activities, directed Milroy to call in his troops, concentrate them at Monterey and take a strong defensive position. He informed his subordinate that Schenck was leaving for Moorefield the next day, and that Blenker's division was on it's way to Moorefield. General Fremont praised Milroy's men for their actions that day, stating that "Your men behaved well. Make them my thanks for it."[19]

On the morning of April 13, Milroy sent out a scouting party, which went a mile beyond McDowell, where there was some skirmishing with the Confederate pickets. At McDowell, the scouts learned from the citizens that Johnson was busily erecting fortifications on Shenandoah Mountain. The citizens reported that Johnson had 3,500 troops there, along with 2,000 negroes working on the fortifications. It is very unlikely that General Johnson had any negroes working on Fort Johnson, as the slave population in that area did not begin to approach that figure. Besides, a large number of the slaves in that area had been detailed to work on the fortifications about Richmond.

When his scouts reported back to Monterey, General Milroy studied the situation a while and remarked, "I will hist them out of that as soon as I get the ballance [sic] of my forces up and get leave from Fremont to advance."[20]

On Sunday morning, April 13, Johnson ordered his troops into their old camp on Shenandoah Mountain. His cavalry was instructed to picket and scout the roads as far as McDowell. On this spring Sabbath, "Alleghany Ed" also could reflect with satisfaction on recent activities. He had attained his objective in forays against the Federals — his men had been under fire, some for the first time, and had not suffered any loss. General Johnson felt sure now that the Federals intended to advance into the Shenandoah Valley, via the Staunton-Parkersburg Turnpike, and planned his defenses accordingly.

Meanwhile at Monterey on April 13, Yankee officers were glancing about apprehensively. An alarm was sounded on receipt of a report that Confederates were advancing from the direction of Crab Bottom (Blue Grass). The 2nd (West) Virginia was sent out to ascertain the truth of the report. When the regiment found that the force under question was composed of blueclad comrades, everybody breathed a sigh of relief.[21]

CHAPTER III
April 14 to 21, 1862

After the skirmish at Monterey on April 12, General Johnson fell back to the fortifications on Shenandoah Mountain. Meanwhile, his cavalry remained at McDowell until April 14, when it fell back to Shaw's Fork, at the western base of Shenandoah Mountain. General Milroy, at Monterey, was anxiously waiting for orders from General Fremont to occupy McDowell.

General Fremont, having received a report from Milroy of the action on April 12, relayed the news to the War Department. The general told Secretary of War Stanton that General Johnson was personally in command of the 1,500 men and two guns involved. To this report, Fremont added somewhat criptically, "I suppose Johnson to mean Jackson."[1] "The Pathfinder" was unaware that Jackson, at that very moment was on the Valley Turnpike near Harrisonburg.

Although the guns of the two armies fell silent temporarily in the third week of April, northern troops were by no means idle. Major Alexander C. Jones, on detached service from the 44th Virginia Infantry, notified Johnson that, on April 15, about 100 Yankees followed the Jackson River into Bath County. At a spot about 14 miles north of Warm Springs, the invaders carried away several wagon loads of grain and bacon. "These marauding visits will probably be repeated,"[2] the V.M.I. graduate prophesied.

As Jones was making his report to Johnson of the Yankee transgressions, General Milroy dispatched a scouting party toward McDowell. The column was led by Company I, 2nd (West) Virginia Infantry. This company, which had been the first Federal unit to enter Monterey, gained further distinction by becoming the first Union company to enter McDowell. Two days later, on April 18, the scouting party returned to Monterey.[3]

Major Jones also was actively engaged in scouting at this time. The officer in command of Confederate forces in Bath County informed General Johnson from Clover Dale that he had placed scouts on roads leading to Scotchtown and Green Valley. Major Jones advised the general further that scouts had been ordered on two paths leading to two gaps named "Pinch-em-Slider [Slidy]" and "Jerk-em-Tight."[4] These mountain trails, Jones added, were extremely rugged and difficult, so much so that a horseman could not pass over them. As a result, Jones's cavalry scouts had to leave their horses about a mile from the Harrisonburg-Warm Springs Turnpike and proceed on foot. It was the Major's opinion that a force

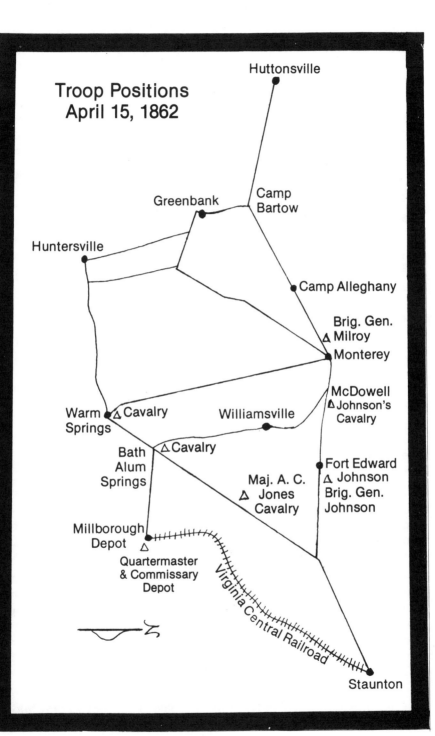

Troop Positions
April 15, 1862

Huttonsville

Greenbank

Camp Bartow

Huntersville

Camp Alleghany

Brig. Gen.
△ Milroy
Monterey

McDowell
△ Johnson's
Cavalry

Warm
Springs △ Cavalry

Williamsville

Bath
Alum
Springs △ Cavalry

Fort Edward
△ Johnson
Brig. Gen.
Johnson

Maj. A. C.
△ Jones
Cavalry

Millborough
Depot
△
Quartermaster
& Commissary
Depot

Virginia Central Railroad

Staunton

of 30 infantrymen, with a mounted courier, could scout this area much more effectively than cavalry. Major Jones also informed Johnson that he was sending scouts beyond Huntersville, to learn the enemy's movements in that area.[5]

The long-awaited junction of Milroy and Schenck occurred finally on April 17, when detachments of both commands entered Franklin, Pendleton County. At the same time Blenker's wandering division was reported in the vicinity of Winchester, still trying to find its way to Moorefield.

That same morning, about 60 Federals approached Johnson's outposts and pickets on the western side of the mountain. After exchanging a few shots, the Confederate pickets fell back, believing they were facing the advance guard of Milroy's main army.

At Fort Johnson the signal gun was fired to sound the alert. At the eastern base of the mountain, the 12th Georgia and 58th Virginia heard the signal and responded quickly, double-timing the four miles to the crest. From there, a column of infantry advanced down the western side of the mountain, quickly learned that it had been only a scouting party, and returned to camp.[6]

From available evidence, it appears that on this date, April 17, a portion of Milroy's troops occupied McDowell. As the Yankees entered the village, a large number of the residents fled, leaving only two families behind. The fine brick home of Felix Hull, whose family had remained, was commandeered for officers quarters.

As the Yankees were entering McDowell, Reverend William T. Price made his way eastward. The clergyman carried word of the occupation to the cavalry camp at Shaw's Fork, where he found the men preparing their evening meals, tending their horses and "all in blissful ignorance" of the advancing enemy.[7]

After being detained for awhile by a group of playful horsemen, who pretended to be the guard, Price found the officer in charge, to whom he broke the news. General Johnson was advised of this development at once.

After dark, Price made his way up the mountain to Fort Johnson. There he found the men busily engaged in reinforcing their pickets, preparing for the enemy should they advance upon them. General Johnson himself was at his headquarters near Mason's Shanties at the mouth of Ramsey's Draft. Here Price revealed full details of the occupation of McDowell, stating that he was of the opinion that it was to be a permanent camp.[8]

Major Alexander C. Jones also was taking steps to meet a Union assault. The 32-year-old native of Moundsville in Marshall County informed Johnson on April 17 that the Bath Cavalry was now scouting all the roads leading toward the enemy.[9]

As the opposing forces jockeyed for position, General William S. Rosecrans outlined a plan of action for the invading army. Writing to the secretary of war on April 18, "Old Rosy" explained:

> After a full consultation with General Banks [I] have concluded to say: Our troops here, east and west, are idle. One brigade added to Fremont's force will do all there if combined with the following: Move [the] rest of Blenker's [division] on Luray, to cut off Jackson's retreat by Thornton's Gap; Banks to move on Harrisonburg; Fremont to follow with forces from Moorefield, supporting with those at Monterey; thence on Staunton or west, according to circumstances, to sustain the corps of Banks; he to move by Staunton or Brown's Gap, to sustain move of the Blenker column toward Culpeper or Standardsville, Madison, or Charlottes[ville] or Gordonsville; McDowell moves up and sustains this advance, with 50,000, to drive them behind the James River, while Fremont, closing in, would threaten to turn that line by Lynchburg.[10]

Secretary Staunton quickly quashed any hopes Roserans may have entertained for the adoption of his scheme. The secretary replied:

> The President will not sanction the plan you propose until it is more fully matured and after full conference and agreement by all who are to participate in it. The Department has no evidence from Fremont, Banks, or McDowell that they have been consulted or will co-operate. When you have obeyed your instructions by placing Blenker's division under General Fremont's orders you will return immediately to Washington and wait orders.[11]

On April 18, Fremont ordered Schenck to move to Franklin and send detachments to Seneca Creek, as well as to the North Fork of the South Branch of the Potomac to crush any guerrilla activities he might encounter. Simultaneously, Schenck was informed that Milroy would assist him from Monterey.[12]

As Schenck prepared to obey his orders, Milroy ascended an eminence about two miles from Fort Johnson. There he obtained an excellent view of the Confederate camp, fortifications and guns. Milroy observed at length and was, in turn, observed by the Rebels, including General Johnson, who recognized his counter-part with the aid of a spyglass. Lieutenant S. L. Williams of the 58th Virginia was inspecting the fortifications when this little tableau was enacted. The officer wrote:

> After being there a while I saw considerable stirring about

among our cavalry pickets on Shaw's Ridge, finally [they] made a dash for camp. Pretty soon I saw, for the first time, a company of wild Yankees make their appearance, [I] could distinctly see the smoke and hear the fire of their guns on our pickets stationed on the advanced post. The balls fell thick around the men, a distance of 500 yards, [they] did no damage. Several of our men [58th Virginia] were on that post, the officers appeared perfectly indifferent all the time the firing was going on. They [the Yankees] never made their appearance after that day that we knew of.[13]

After Fort Johnson was abandoned, Milroy surmised that Johnson had withdrawn out of fear of an attack.[14]

As long as the Confederates occupied Fort Johnson, Milroy felt that it was impossible for him to advance on the Staunton-Parkersburg Turnpike. He was about to select an alternate route when the Rebels vacated the mountain. General Milroy learned of the evacuation late on April 19 and, according to Reverend Price, "evidently regarded the 'on to Staunton' as virtually accomplished, when the stars and stripes floated from the wooden walls of the temporary confederate fortifications on Shenandoah summit."[15]

Now that Milroy and Schenck were for all general purposes united, Fremont speculated on an early arrival of Blenker. Where was the German revolutionary and his 10,000 troops? The report was unfavorable. According to Rosecrans, Blenker still was near Winchester, his men in dire need of tents, shoes and forage. Nor had they been paid for a long time.

That being the state of affairs, Fremont urged Stanton to provision the troops immediately and issue back pay. Once those deficiencies were corrected, Fremont ordered Blenker to march toward Moorefield.[16]

General Milroy, who had been reinforced by three regiments, including the 73rd Ohio, received the following message from Fremont on April 20:

It was not expected when you were directed to move forward that re-enforcements for the department would be so long delayed or your advance would have been postponed. Reports from various sources all indicate a concentration of the enemy's forces and an attack upon our most exposed position. Under these circumstances you will not move forward until specially directed to do so. Meantime keep your communication with General Schenck open.[17]

It is unclear whether Fremont prohibited Milroy's advance from Monterey or McDowell. According to communications of April 18 and 20 it appears that Fremont believed him to be at Monterey and indicates that

Milroy advanced to McDowell without instructions from the department chief.

While Fremont was mapping strategy in the hills of Highland County, Stonewall Jackson was pursuing a leisurely course up the Valley Turnpike following his defeat at Kernstown on March 23.

The Valley Army was at Stony Creek on April 16 when, in the early morning hours, enemy cavalry crossed the stream and captured Captain Addison Harper's cavalry company still sleeping soundly. Due to either a false sense of security or sheer negligence, Harper's cavalry did not post any guards. More than 50 Rebel cavalrymen were captured near Columbia Furnace, along with their horses, baggage and equipment.[18]

Once General Jackson became aware of the capture of Harper's men, he believed that Blenker's division had reinforced Banks, and he pulled back his advance infantry forces to Rude's Hill. This left Colonel Turner Ashby in command of the rear guard, which Jackson ordered to abandon Stony Creek only if attacked.

The attack was made before dawn on April 17. As ordered, Ashby fell back, pausing only long enough on the way to destroy railroad property in Mount Jackson.

Now only one barrier remained between Jackson and the pursuing Federals. It was the bridge over the North Fork of the Shenandoah River south of Mount Jackson. When the last cavalryman crossed over the bridge, Captain John Q. Winfield was ordered to set fire to the structure. As the blaze caught up, Captain Winfield and his men blocked the bridge, preparing to open fire on the advancing Federals. At the last moment Captain Winfield ordered his men to commence firing, driving the blueclad cavalrymen back, but only for a moment. This time the Federal troopers managed to cross the burning bridge, stamping out the flames and rushed Ashby's command. The fighting was now at close quarters, and only through the valiant efforts of his men did Colonel Ashby escape capture. More and more Federal squadrons dashed across the still smoldering bridge, and Ashby's cavalry were scattered for the first time, falling back to Rude's Hill.[19]

From here the Army of the Valley retired to Harrisonburg and then marched in an easterly direction. On the evening of April 19, Jackson went into camp at Swift Run Gap near Conrad's Store, now known as the town of Elkton. The position here was an excellent defensive one, as there was only one approach to guard.[20]

Before arriving at his camp at the foot of the Blue Ridge, Jackson sent a message to General Richard S. Ewell, directing that officer to bring his division from Brandy Station toward Swift Run Gap.[21]

On April 18, Robert E. Lee directed Edward Johnson on Shenandoah

21

Mountain to watch Jackson's movements in the Valley and to coordinate his actions with them. "If he is compelled to retire to Swift Run Gap," Lee wrote from Richmond, "it will be necessary for you to move to Staunton; and should you find the enemy marching in too strong force for you to resist upon that place [Staunton], you must retire toward Waynesborough. . ."[22]

General Jackson, too, was in communication with Johnson. The commander of the Valley Army asked Johnson to meet him at his camp near Harrisonburg. General Johnson left Shenandoah Mountain about 6 a.m. on the morning of April 19, leaving the senior colonel in command, and arrived at Jackson's headquarters that night.[23]

General Johnson had not been gone very long when the colonel commanding issued orders for the men to prepare to abandon their position on Shenandoah Mountain. The tents were ordered to be struck, trunks were to be burned and the men were to take only what clothing they could carry on their backs. The work of striking camp had hardly begun, when the colonel countermanded that order and directed that the tents and trunks were to be burned. The men were to salvage what clothing they could carry.[24] The tents were burned, and a quantity of quartermaster and commissary stores were destroyed. During the confusion, many of the discontented militia deserted and returned to their homes. The withdrawal was begun amid a heavy downpour about 2 p.m. on the afternoon of April 19.[25]

William T. Price termed the evacuation a surprise to both armies. The fortifications on Shenandoah Mountain, he said, were "one of the strongest holds in the Southern Confederacy, and in some respects one of the most important in holding West Virginia."[26]

S. L. Williams of the 58th Virginia expressed regret at leaving the mountain stronghold. The lieutenant wrote: "I am sorry we had to leave Camp Shenandoah. Oh, it was a magnificent place, good water, good camping, the healthiest place we have been, as yet. . . . We were well fortified, having 12 pieces of cannon, well arranged."[27]

Reverend Price believed that the evacuation of Fort Johnson was caused by panic in Staunton. According to a popular rumor, an unidentified quartermaster in Staunton had heard that Jackson had ordered the evacuation of the Augusta County community and that the town was to be occupied by the Federals. As a result, Confederate sick and wounded were placed on trains and shipped to Gordonsville. In addition, the local bank and court records were shipped to Charlottesville.[28]

A dispatch was sent to Shenandoah Mountain stating that the Yankees were expected at Staunton by a certain time. If the garrison at Shenandoah Mountain would fall back to Buffalo Gap in time, they could

22

escape capture by going to Staunton or Waynesboro. If they did not reach Buffalo Gap in time, they could find another escape route, and join the Valley Army.

The senior colonel, who was un-named in Price's account (either Colonel George A. Porterfield or Colonel John B. Baldwin), had access to the order from Richmond to General Johnson concerning the retreat from Alleghany Mountain. The colonel took particular note of the portion of the order which gave the commanding officer the discretion of not occupying Shenandoah Mountain. This, coupled with the information from Staunton, the colonel felt that it was folly to remain at Fort Johnson.

Instead of the order relating to the retreat from Alleghany Mountain, it is possible that the letter from General Lee arrived after General Johnson had left for Jackson's camp. This letter gave specific instructions to Johnson to fall back to Staunton if Jackson was compelled to fall back to Swift Run Gap. The senior colonel left in command would be privy to the information that Jackson was headed for Swift Run Gap, and would take it upon himself to follow General Lee's instructions.

Captain S. G. Pryor of the 12th Georgia remembered that the march to Buffalo Gap was over the worst roads he had ever seen. Captain Prior wrote that he had to wade through mud up to his knees, and that they arrived at Buffalo Gap about midnight. Fires were kindled and offered some measure of comfort in the constant downpour. The weary men of Johnson's army remained here until late in the afternoon of April 20, when they marched to West View and Valley Mills. At West View they received orders to halt until new orders could be given.[29]

It had been a painful experience for Johnson's troops. Rain fell in torrents, soaking their clothing and blankets, and the frigid winds cut through them like knives. There was virtually no shelter, except what could be improvised from boards, fence rails and cedar boughs or was provided by stables, sheds, homes and vacant cellars.[30]

When Milroy learned of the Confederate evacuation of Shenandoah Mountain, he ordered six infantry companies and one cavalry company to pursue the enemy. At Fort Johnson, the Yankees found signs of the hasty departure. Vast quantities of flour and forage had been destroyed. Tents that were not burned had been slashed so badly that they were useless.[31]

About ten miles beyond the camp, near Buffalo Gap, the bluecoats encountered Johnson's rear guard. A lively skirmish ensued before the Unionist called off the fight.

General Milroy, as he had done previously, bemoaned the lack of orders to advance. He wrote:

Had I have had my whole force with me as I should have
had and would have had if not restrained by positive orders I

23

would have pitched into them, clearing the way for and dashed into Staunton where I have been trying to get for six months and where we ought to have been five months ago.[32]

The Federals, according to General Milroy, remained in the Buffalo Gap area for several days, skirmishing frequently with the Rebels. The general reported that during this period several hundred Confederates entered the Union lines. The deserters, Milroy said, were given the oath of allegiance and permitted to return to their homes.

General Edward Johnson, after conferring with Jackson at Swift Run Gap, left for his command, which he supposed was still at Shenandoah Mountain.[33] On his way back, Johnson was greatly surprised to learn that his troops had abandoned their position on Shenandoah Mountain. The next day, April 21, Johnson reorganized his army, dividing it into two brigades. One was commanded by Colonel George Alexander Porterfield, a 39-year-old graduate of V.M.I. and a veteran of the Mexican War. It consisted of the 12th Georgia, the 25th and 31st Virginia Infantry Regiments, George W. Hansbrough's Battalion of Infantry and the Star Battery. The other brigade was commanded by Colonel John Brown Baldwin, a 42-year-old lawyer from Staunton and member of the Virginia Legislature. It was comprised of the 44th, 52nd and 58th Virginia Regiments, plus Miller's and Lee's Batteries.[34]

In Washington, meanwhile, Lincoln was growing impatient over Fremont's inactivity. On April 21, the department commander received a telegram from the War Department reading: "The President desires to know when you intend to move toward Knoxville, and with what force and by what route, and whether you contemplate any co-operation with [General Ormsby McK.] Mitchel."[35]

General Fremont replied immediately. He explained that his original intention was to guard the Baltimore and Ohio Railroad and loyal citizens with 10,000 men. Next he wanted to send 25,000 men by rail to Kentucky and then march them into Tennessee. But, Fremont added, "difficulties, however, in the way of obtaining the requisite number of troops have led to a change of my plan."[36] He outlined his new plan as follows:

> The first base of operations being the Baltimore and Ohio Railroad, the division of General Blenker, which, from the best information I can obtain, numbers about 9,000 men, will take position at Moorefield. At this point or at Franklin it will unite with the troops now under command of General Schenck, numbering about 3,000. With these, acting in conjunction with General Banks, I propose to move up the valley of Virginia by a course which you will see on the accompanying map, over roads which are as dry and as good at all seasons of the year as any in Virginia, and through a country where forage is easily ob-

tained. At Monterey I shall be joined by the troops under General Milroy, numbering, 3,500 effective men and can then strike the railroad at or near Salem, while General Cox with his 7,000 men takes possession of Newbern, or can first effect a junction with General Cox, and seize the railraod with a force then increased to about 22,000.[37]

The War Department approved of Fremont's proposal, but with some modifications. After striking the railroad near Salem, he was ordered not to advance toward Knoxville without further instructions. Moreover, he was cautioned "not to consider the movements and position of Banks as being subject to your control."[38]

In another communique to the War Department, Fremont reported that Schenck had been ordered to Franklin, but his progress had been slowed by high waters and the lack of a pontoon train.

CHAPTER IV
April 22 to May 1, 1862

After the Confederates abandoned Shenandoah Mountain, General Robert H. Milroy ordered a detachment of infantry and cavalry to pursue the retreating Rebels.[1] The Yankees overtook the graycoats about six miles from Buffalo Gap, near the Virginia Central Railroad. On April 23, in an engagement about ten miles from Shenandoah Mountain, the Federals killed three of Johnson's men and took two others prisoner. One captive belonged to the Churchville Cavalry, the other was an officer of the 31st Virginia.[2]

While Generals Johnson and Milroy were playing hide and seek in the hills west of Staunton, Stonewall Jackson and Nathaniel P. Banks were playing a game of their own in the Shenandoah Valley. When Jackson went into camp below Swift Run Gap, Banks was not far behind. Harrisonburg was occupied by Federal cavalry on April 22 which was followed a few days later by the divisions of Alpheus Williams and James Shields. The remainder of Banks's command was at New Market.

William S. Rosecrans was busy, too. On April 23, he telegraphed Secretary of War Edward M. Stanton that he planned to take Blenker's division to Moorefield without the least delay. More important, "Old Rosy" offered another scheme to clear the Shenandoah Valley, writing:

> A clearing of the valley and concentration of Fremont toward Staunton and on the railroad; Banks to incline over east and seize the Piedmont and threaten or take Gordonsville and the Kanawha Valley; to seize Lewisburg and support the forces breaking the Southwestern Virginia and Tennessee Railroad; interior movements contingent, but tending to mass the troops as much as requisite to supply each other and subsist. For goodness' sake order the plan of supplies proposed. No man of experience, knowing the people and country, can fail to improve it.[3]

What became of Rosecrans's latest scheme is not stated in the Official Records, and it can be safely assumed that it was disregarded. The next communication between Stanton and the general took place on April 24. In it, Stanton asked only what orders Rosecrans had received from General Fremont regarding his plans for Blenker's division.[4]

As Rosecrans awaited a positive response to his proposal, General Milroy turned his attention to a fresh supply of forage for his horses. On

26

April 24 Lieutenant J. Q. Barnes of the 73rd Ohio was detailed to take 65 men and three wagons down the Jackson River into southern Highland and northern Bath Counties, an area rich in corn and oats.

A few hours after Lieutenant Barnes and his party departed it was dcided to send additional wagons after him. Accordingly, Sergeant Isaac C. Nelson, also of the 73rd Ohio, was placed in charge of 16 wagons, with one man detailed from each company of the regiment as a guard for the train. Sergeant Nelson was ordered to join Barnes, but was sent in the opposite direction from the route taken by that officer.

On the second day out, Nelson led his train through a series of turns that he felt necessary to bring the foraging parties together. The farther he went, however, the more anxious Nelson became. He was on an obscure mountain road and there was a genuine fear that Rebels, or even bushwhackers, lurked around the next corner. Sergeant Nelson halted his wagons and walked on ahead. Beyond the sight of his comrades, he met a stranger on horseback. The sergeant inquired about a route to Williamsville, a small village in northern Bath County. The horseman gave the required directions and asked Nelson if he was a soldier. The sergeant, in full Federal regalia, admitted he was, only to learn that the mounted man mistook him for a Confederate. He was warneḍ to be careful in Williamsville because the town was full of Yankees.

After ascertaining that the nearest Confederate troops were at Bath Alum Springs, 11 miles away, Nelson and the horseman parted company. The citizen, who was exempt from military duty because of having only one eye, is believed to have been the son of Robert Wallace. The younger Wallace was arrested subsequently and brought before Milroy, charged with being a member of the Bath Cavalry.[5]

At Nelson's signal, his wagon train moved forward and made its way to Williamsville. There Nelson learned that two other foraging expeditions were in the neighborhood. That night Nelson and his guard bivouacked in a log schoolhouse. The teamsters spent the night along the Cow Pasture River.

Meanwhile, a citizen of the area, reported to have been John T. Byrd, slipped away to the Rockbridge Alum Springs, where the Bath Cavalry was encamped. Conditions in Williamsville were divulged to the officer in charge, whereupon Lieutenant Andrew S. Brinkley and 40 cavalrymen were ordered to Williamsville. Because the Confederates were under the impression that they were about to clash with a force of approximately 80 men, it was decided that an ambush was the most effective way to attack the train. In that mood, they set out shortly after midnight on April 26. Taking concealment in the laurel thickets on each side of the road, they settled down to await the arrival of the Yankees.

Darkness turned to daylight without incident. As the Confederates waited anxiously, one of the two foraging parties out of McDowell returned to camp, loaded with forage. Undoubtedly, it had passed the laurel thickets before the Bath Cavalry went into position. As a result Nelson's train of 16 wagons and another of nine wagons in charge of the brigade quartermaster remained south of McDowell. For their mutual protection, Nelson and the quartermaster combined their trains. Next, they loaded their wagons with all possible haste and set out for camp. The quartermaster assumed command of the wagons, Nelson of the guard, and ten of them.

With their wagons loaded, the foragers planned to ford the Bull Pasture River at Williamsville and follow the most direct route home. When they were advised by local citizens, however, that recent rains had swelled the river beyond the fording stage, Nelson and his colleague accepted the opinion without question and took another road leading through a ravine — the same roadway on which the Bath Cavalry lay in ambush.

As Nelson and Frank Esker walked ahead of the procession by about 75 yards, a shot rang out. Nelson presumed it was fired by one of the ten guards of the 25-wagon train, aimed perhaps at a rabbit or pheasant. Turning, he saw a puff of smoke on the opposide of the ravine, and knew for certain that the train was under attack when he was struck by a bullet.[6]

Within minutes the foraging party was surrounded by Rebels. At the first sign of the attack, however, some teamsters cut loose their horses, enabling a few men to escape and return to McDowell, where they spread word of their misadvanture at Williamsville. Subsequently, it was revealed that the ambush could have been avoided if Nelson and others had checked the depth of the Bull Pasture River. Instead of being impassable, the water was only "belly deep." The foragers had been duped by the citizens in a most flagrant manner.[7]

When the foragers totaled up their casualties in the ambush, they found two dead, five wounded (three of whom were also taken prisoner) and six additional prisoners.[8] Ironically the two men killed were father and son, Daniel and William Howe, both being shot through the head.

Private Thomas J. Walker, son-in-law of Daniel Howe, although injured, was able to make his way to McDowell, where he announced the fate of the foraging train. The news caused great excitement in the camp.[9]

Another wounded Federal was Frank Esker of the 73rd Ohio, who had been walking with Nelson ahead of the foraging train. He fell into the hands of the Bath Cavalry and was placed in a nearby home to recover. Other prisoners, together with the 80 horses and mules captured in the ravine, were sent to Rockbridge Alum Springs. Later they were transferred to Lexington and then to Staunton. Ultimately, the men were sent to Richmond, where they were imprisoned briefly.[10]

The wagons captured at Williamsville were put to the torch, but only the hay and canvas tops were consumed by the flames. As a result, the running gears of the wagons remained intact and would be usable to the Federal troops that were expected momentarily. Consequently, a member of the Bath Cavalry volunteered to remain behind and see to the destruction of the wagons. Assisted by youths of the vicinity, the spokes were chopped from the wheels and the tongues were cut off the wagons with axes and hatchets. When the chores were completed, the remnants were shoved off the side of the road and into the ravine. Then the group took to its collective heels. It was none to soon, for as they disappeared from view, Captain Shuman's Company of cavalry arrived on the scene and viewed the destruction.[11]

In the days following the Confederate exit from Fort Johnson on Shenandoah Mountain, citizens in the surrounding countryside lived in dread of a Yankee invasion that was expected at any moment. At Millboro Depot on the Virginia Central Railroad, Captain Thomas H. Tutwiler, the quartermaster there, sent all his stores across the mountain to Lexington. Major A. C. Jones, who visited Millboro Depot on April 25, advised General Johnson that all the stores would be removed within 24 hours. The major revealed further that Yankee parties had been spotted at Clover Dale and near Warm Springs and that he had sent scouts along all the roads in the direction of the enemy.[12]

As the Federals sorrowed over the loss of their foraging train, steps were underway to dispose of the Confederates in their front. When the War Department informed Banks of Fremont's plan of action, the New Englander replied, "I shall cooperate with Fremont with great pleasure. Suggested it to him two days since."[13]

General Milroy, too, was advising Washington authorities of developments in his mountainous realm. On April 26, he reported that militiamen who had been drafted into Confederate service were deserting by the hundreds. The general reported that they were taking the oath of allegiance and returning to their homes. The Hoosier lawyer informed his superiors, an 18-inch snowfall and high waters had disrupted communications with General Schenck,[14] who arrived in Petersburg on April 27 with 2,400 men.

In addition to the natural phenomena of the McDowell-Monterey sector, Milroy directed his attention to his artillery, which consisted of only two sections. To strenghten this arm, the general dispatched Captain Ewing to Elkwater to bring up a six-gun battery. Hire or impress whatever teams were necessary to haul the guns, the captain was told. By the first week in May, the chore was completed.[15]

In other actions of late April, General Milroy advanced some troops to within seven miles of Staunton and reported to Fremont that Edward Johnson was still retreating and was believed on his way to join Jackson in the Shenandoah Valley. General Fremont passed this information on to Secretary of War Stanton, plus the additional intelligence that a foraging train had been attacked nearby. The general also communicated to the secretary that troops had been detached to Williamsville to suppress the guerrillas, that the streams between Moorefield and Franklin remained impassable and that he expected Blenker's sluggish division to arrive in Moorefield very shortly.[16]

The delegation that General Milroy ordered to Williamsville to deal with those who were responsible for the attack on the foraging train consisted of 250 men under the command of Major Richard Long of the 73rd Ohio. That officer was ordered "to destroy the town if I found that the citizens had assisted in the destruction of the train or if the guerrillas had been harbored or assisted there and to kill all guerrillas that I could capture and hang their bodies by the roadside as a warning."[17]

Major Long began his mission on the morning of April 28. With him were Companies A, C and G of his regiment. In late afternoon the contingent went into camp four miles beyond McDowell. When Long resumed his march at 7 o'clock the next morning, his command was substantially larger than at the beginning. A small cavalry force had joined up along the way and, in addition, the major had impressed wagons and horses to replace those lost at Williamsville.

Major Long arrived at Williamsville at 3 o'clock on the afternoon of April 29. He surveyed the wagon wreckage and from it reconstructed six vehicles. By 6 p.m. the Federals occupied the town, where they found only two male inhabitants.[18]

The next morning Long directed two lieutenants to continue to "capture" horses and wagons. Some troops were sent south of the village to take possession of two flour mills. Others were assigned to Williamsville to maintain law and order. Part of this force was detailed to repair the wagons recovered from the ravine and to operate the mill in Williamsville.

As the Yankees were exacting reparations from the townsfolk on May 1, Major Long was alerted to the approach of enemy cavalry seven miles away. An attack was imminent, he was told. To that bit of intelligence, a free negro added the disquieting news that a large body of infantry had reinforced the Confederate cavalry.

The bad tidings spurred Major Long into instant action. He notified General Milroy of the mounting danger and requested additional troops. While waiting the general's reply, Long dispatched scouting parties to learn further details. The major himself led one group toward Warm Springs. No signs of the Rebels were spotted there. When a second detachment reported similiarly on another road, Long concluded that the graycoats had fallen back. After the major was reinforced by Companies F and I of the 2nd (West) Virginia Infantry, and a company of the 1st (West) Virginia Cavalry, he noted, "I can now hold this place."[19]

More scouting parties took to the roads on May 2, patrolling toward Bath Alum and Warm Springs. Again there were no traces of Rebels, whereupon Long wrote, "I decided to go down with a force of infantry and cavalry, but upon consultation with the officers it was thought best to return to McDowell as our troops were needed there."[20]

The return march commenced at 10 a.m. on May 4. Six hours later the major arrived at McDowell. The train consisted not only of many wagons loaded with flour, but also six prisoners identified only as Swope, Hedger, Lange, Parmer, Dill, Wallace and Mcclintic.[21] In all probability, Wallace was the same individual whom Sergeant Nelson had met while en route to Williamsville several days before.

During Major Long's absence from camp General Milroy was reinforced by the 73rd and 75th Ohio, and in all likelihood, by two other regiments from Monterey. As a result of this exodus, only a few companies remained behind to guard Monterey.

In late April, the Federals were beginning to strengthen their forces at Fredericksburg. This meant pulling troops from some other point — most likely the Valley. Once that happened, then it would be a good time for Jackson to make a move.

On April 27, Colonel Turner Ashby reported to General Jackson that he was falling back before a superior force under Banks, who was then holding Harrisonburg. The Yankees were only seven miles from Jackson's encampment at Swift Run Gap and skirmished briskly with Ashby. Union sources revealed that Banks had suffered only two casualties, both shot accidentally. The Confederates had five killed and as many wounded.[22]

The stage was now set for Jackson to launch his dramatic Valley Campaign, and he proposed three scenarios for the consideration of General Robert E. Lee. They were:

1 — Order Dick Ewell's division from Brandy Station to Swift Run Gap to threaten Banks should the Federals move on Staunton, while Jackson led his own division toward McDowell and, with Edward Johnson's small force, dispose of Milroy.

2 — Unite with Ewell and attack Banks between New Market and the Shenandoah River. If successful, then strike Bank's rear at New Market, compelling him to fall back.

3 — Move to Sperryville and threaten Winchester via Front Royal,

again causing Banks to fall back.

Of the three proposals, Jackson favored the first and expressed his opinion to Lee. "If I receive an answer justifying a move in that direction," he told Lee, "I may leave here to-morrow via Port Republic."[23]

General Lee replied to Jackson's letter on May 1, informing his subordinate that the choice of actions was Jackson's to make. It was well that Lee responded as he did, because on the day of his reply Jackson was already on the move. He was one day out of camp. Ewell's men were occupying Jackson's old campground, and Stonewall's division was struggling through ankle-deep mud headed toward Port Republic. General Milroy was his target.

In preparation for the campaign, Jackson had sent Jed Hotchkiss, his topographical engineer, to confer with Edward Johnson at Valley Mills, a few miles beyond Staunton. Hotchkiss's errand: To learn from Johnson how best to deal with Milroy. Hotchkiss reported back to Jackson on April 29, a day before Jackson broke camp.[24]

Banks was instantly and fully aware of Jackson's exodus from Swift Run Gap. But where was he going? Banks was thoroughly mystified. He was certain Jackson was on his way to Richmond to reinforce the Army of Northern Virginia that was contesting George B. McClellan's advance on the capital of the Confederacy. "This is the fact, I have no doubt," the general assured authorities in Washington.[25]

General Jackson not only misled Banks, he also misled his own men. From Port Republic, the Valley Army marched eastward through Brown's Gap in the Blue Ridge. Confidence mushroomed in the ranks. The men were certain that Richmond was their destination. Down the eastern slope of the Blue Ridge they trudged into Albemarle County and toward Mechum's River Station on the Virginia Central Railroad. The Virginia Central would carry them to Richmond. Of that there was no doubt. But surprise of surprises, the locomotives that awaited them with steam up, were facing the Shenandoah Valley. Suddenly, Jackson's strategy was perfectly clear. He had left the Valley only to confuse Union spies in the neighborhood. The general's quarry was Milroy in the rugged terrain around McDowell.

While Jackson was maneuvering back and forth across the Blue Ridge, Johnson's men received orders to prepare to march at a moment's notice.[26] The reason for this unusual order was not explained, but was probably due to the many disturbing rumors circulating at that time.

Before leaving Swift Run Gap, Jackson wrote to Francis H. Smith, superintendent of the Virginia Military Institute, where Jackson had taught for the 10 years prior to the war. In his letter, Jackson requested that Smith bring the Corps of Cadets to Staunton "... if you feel authoriz-

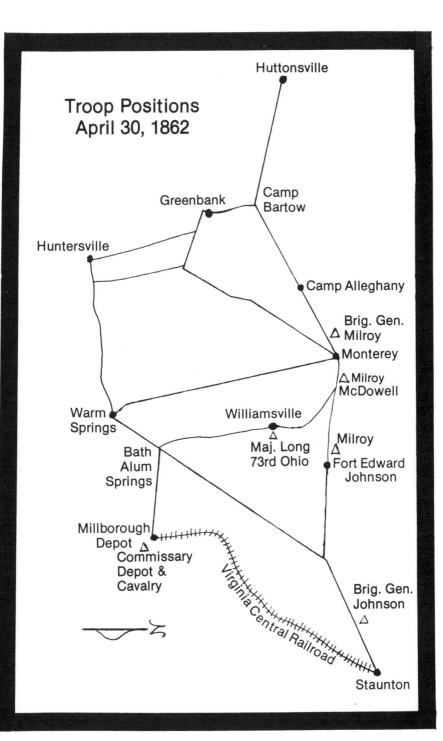

Troop Positions
April 30, 1862

Huttonsville

Camp Bartow

Greenbank

Huntersville

Camp Alleghany

Brig. Gen.
△ Milroy
Monterey

△ Milroy
McDowell

Warm Springs

Williamsville

Milroy
△

△ Maj. Long
73rd Ohio

Fort Edward Johnson

Bath
Alum
Springs

Millborough
Depot △
Commissary
Depot &
Cavalry

Brig. Gen.
Johnson
△

Virginia Central Railroad

Staunton

ed to cooperate in an important movement which I will explain to you when we meet."[27]

It was Jackson's intention for the Cadets to serve as guards of his trains, thereby freeing regular troops for the anticipated battle that he was sure lay ahead.

Early on May 1, Smith addressed the Cadets. He told the young men: "I want no cadet to accompany the command except those who feel that they go with the consent of their parents, either presumed or actual."[28]

With that, four companies of Cadets marched out of Lexington under the command of Major Scott Shipp. Remaining behind to guard the Institute and the arsenal were only 11 Cadets.

The Federals also were planning for action. On May 11, Fremont assured Stanton that:

> The plan of operations which the President approved is now being carried into effect. Obstacles of weather, floods, and deficient transportation are being overcome, and all movements made in reference to it."[29]

General Milroy shared Fremont's high state of optimism. The Indianan informed his superior that, according to scouts, deserters and refugees, Edward Johnson's command was at West View and "ready to retreat upon any advance by us."[30]

In the meantime, with his whereabouts uncertain, Jackson was no longer a grave concern of Lincoln and Stanton. On May 1 the War Department ordered Banks to withdraw from Harrisonburg and fall back to Strasburg, or another strong position near there. General Banks also was ordered to send the division of James Shields to Fredericksburg, further depleting Union numbers in the Shenandoah Valley.

CHAPTER V

May 2 to May 6, 1862

General Robert H. Milroy's swift retaliation against the Williamsville guerrillas elicited lofty commendation from John C. Fremont. On May 2, the commander of the Mountain Department wrote to the 46-year-old brigadier:

> Your efforts in suppression of guerrillas approved. The commanding general takes this occasion to say that he has been gratified with the good conduct and gallantry displayed by your command since entering the Monterey Valley, and requests that as much be conveyed to them through your headquarters. He also desires me to say that special thanks are due to yourself for the vigilant activity you have shown in keeping yourself so thoroughly acquainted with the movements of the enemy.[1]

While earning the laudation of Fremont, Milroy also incurred the extreme enmity of the Confederates. In particular, he was loathed because of his measures against the Williamsville miscreants and, it was said, a reward had been offered for him dead or alive.[2]

To a lesser degree, Jackson also was on the minds of the Valley inhabitants. They felt that they had been forsaken, that they had been left to the ravages of the invaders when Jackson marched over the Blue Ridge. Anxiety ruled Union sympathizers. Where would "Old Jack" strike next?

By May 2, Nathaniel Banks had an idea where Jackson's next blow would fall. On that date the ex-governor of Massachusetts wired Fremont that Jackson was moving "possibly to join Johnson and attack Milroy near Staunton."[3]

Two days later Milroy was advised of the possiblity and was urged to be on the alert for a likely attack.

By this time Jackson was not the only one in motion. General Robert C. Schenck, the crackerjack poker player from Ohio, had advanced to within 11 miles of Franklin and 30 miles of Milroy. General Schenck entered Franklin on May 5.

Nor was Milroy stationary. With three regiments of infantry, a battery of artillery and a company of cavalry, he crossed the Shenandoah Mountain and camped within 15 miles of Staunton. Left behind at McDowell were three regiments, three batteries and two cavalry companies.[4]

General Milroy's command now consisted of the 25th, 32nd, 73rd and 75th Ohio Regiments, the 2nd and 3rd (West) Virginia Regiments, Battery I, 1st Ohio, 12th Ohio Independent Battery, Battery G, 1st (West) Virginia, and Companies C, E and L of the 1st (West) Virginia Cavalry.[5]

From his position in Brown's Gap, Jackson laid the groundwork for the engagement that he knew was sure to come. On May 3, he wrote to Francis H. Smith, asking the V.M.I. superintendent to utilize whatever free time he had to familiarize himself with the country west of Staunton. Stonewall wrote: "I desire all the information possible respecting the military features of the country between us and the enemy."[6]

Meanwhile, Edward Johnson wired Jackson, urging the major general "to come up as soon as possible."[7] General Johnson also sent a message through his ranks, asking for volunteers to form a scouting party from his position at West View. The general sought information on the rear of Milroy's army.

Fourteen men from that section of the state stepped forward. They were members of the 25th and 31st Virginia and knew the area intimately. Each man was issued 40 rounds of ammunition before they left camp on May 4 under the leadership of Captains Harden and Lang.

Late in the evening the delegation struck the Bull Pasture River. Here the scouts were unsure of their route. Their quandary was resolved when Private John Jehu Trainer, who grew up in Highland County, offered to lead the way.

Four miles north of McDowell the group came to the Botkin home, where they spent the night. The next morning the scouts were awakened by the sound of gunfire and horses pounding down the road. Trainer maintained that the horsemen were members of the Bath Cavalry and were in full retreat. In this assertion, Trainer was probably incorrect as there is no record of Confederate troopers being detailed for service in this area. Furthermore, the Bath Cavalry was busy south of McDowell at this time, keeping watch over Milroy's foragers.

From their overnight refuge, Trainer and his companions crossed Jack Mountain and proceeded to the fork of the Monterey and Jackson River roads. Crossing the Jackson River, the Rebel scouts moved along the side of the McNulty Mountains. The approach of Federal infantry, on its way from Huntersville to join Milroy, temporarily halted the party's progress. When the march was resumed, the graycoats climbed Monterey Mountain. On the top, Dr. David B. Lang surveyed the surrounding countryside through his telescope and obtained the information requested by Johnson.

Late that evening it was decided that Harden and Lang would retain three men on the mountain top, while the remainder of the group, led by

Trainer, would return to West View and report their findings to Johnson.

The return trek was interrupted once near the Monterey road. Six union cavalrymen challenged Trainer's party and fired upon the men, bringing down one of them. Following a night at the home of Louis Davis, Trainer led his charges into Johnson's camp on May 6.[8]

During the scouts' foray into the mountains, a new wave of excitement had engulfed the townspeople of Staunton. On Sunday, May 4, steam locomotives had rolled in from the east. From their cars leaped hordes of gray-clad Valley men. They were members of Jackson's army, freshly arrived from Mechum's River Station in the final act of Jackson's maneuver to confuse the enemy. The troops camped two miles east of town.

On hand to greet Jackson was Francis H. Smith and 200 Cadets from V.M.I. Although Jackson had ordered Smith to bring the Cadets to Staunton, his course had not been without impediments. Before acceding to Jackson's request, Smith asked permission from the Board of Visitors to subject the embryonic soldiers to the fury of combat. The reply was not long in coming. It was unanimous — an unqualified no, unless the Institute was in jeopardy.

On receipt of the decision, Smith fired off a dispatch to Governor John Letcher in Richmond. The superintendent said he would abide by the board's decision "unless otherwise directed."[9]

After reading Smith's message from Staunton, the governor answered: "I do not see how the cadets can be sent back. I think it best to let them go on. The mischief is done and we shall have to let it alone."[10]

General Smith also reported his predicament to Jackson and was relieved to read the general's response in which he said, "The safety of this section of the Valley, in my opinion, renders your continued cooperation of great importance."[11]

General Jackson's posture elicited Smith's full approval. He advised "Stonewall" that his statement ". . . removed all doubt from my mind as to my duty to give you that cooperation with the limitation of excluding all cadets under eighteen years of age, who have not the consent of their parents to participate in this temporary service."[12]

In his continuing efforts to learn everything that could be known about the country in which he proposed to clash with the enemy, Jackson directed Jed Hotchkiss and Colonel Thomas H. Williamson, on leave from V.M.I., to report to General Johnson at West View. The pair conferred with Johnson without delay. On the morning of May 5, they set out on their mission with an escort of cavalry and Captain R. D. Lilley's company (D) of the 25th Virginia Infantry Regiment. The party passed Big North Mountain and turned northeast at Dry Branch Gap, following the crest of Crawford

Mountain. Some distance later they spotted the Federal encampment near Ramsey's Draft. From their vantage point, Hotchkiss and Williamson recorded their observations which were presented to Johnson upon their return to camp.[13]

The next morning, Hotchkiss and Williamson returned to Crawford Mountain for further study. To their surprise, all traces of the Yankees were gone. The two advised Johnson of the development, and also informed Jackson that the Federals had pulled back and that Johnson was advancing.[14]

The whirlwind of rumors that invariably surrounds military activity in wartime ensnared the citizens of Bath County in early May. A report that Yankees were in Green Valley, on the Harrisonburg-Warm Springs Turnpike and were preparing to attack Millboro Depot, the western-most station on the Virginia Central, galvanized the citizenry into action. A band of rangers was organized about May 6, to deal with the supposed threat. It was commanded by Reverend William T. Price, a circuit rider in Bath and Highland Counties. A company of cavalry, commanded by a Lieutenant Potts, accompanied the "Rangers".[15]

Hoping to ambush their northern tormenters, the two groups set out toward a previously agreed upon spot near midnight. Three miles from their destination, a halt was ordered and the horses taken out of sight. By daylight the "Rangers" were in position and ready for whatever came their way.

Very shortly a local farmer informed the "Rangers" that no Federals had been seen in the vicinity for several days. Price and his men held their ground. Later, a second individual suggested that the "Rangers" move to a more suitable ground. At first the "Rangers" disregarded the recommendation. After the departure of the second informant, the "Rangers" altered their lines slightly, not trusting the man.

The wait at the new location was soon rewarded. Soon after reaching their new position a group of horsemen were seen at the Green Valley house. The horsemen halted a moment, then rode toward Price's men. There was no doubt in the minds of the Southeners that these were Yankees. Rifles were raised, but no trigger was pulled. The rifles were lowered because, even to an untrained eye, it was apparent that the "Rangers" were badly outnumbered. It would be sheer folly to engage the horsemen in combat. The "Rangers" fell back to higher ground where it was discovered that a horrible blunder had been narrowly averted. The horsemen were Confederate cavalry who had ridden out to inform the "Rangers" that no danger existed.

Back at the Green Valley house, Reverend Price and Alexander Caldwell Jones, now a lieutenant colonel, held a conference. A map of the area was spread out on the table before them. Colonel Jones had been ordered by General Jackson to make a demonstration in the direction of Williamsville to draw Federal "attention from the movement of General Ed. Johnson & Jackson, against Milroy's forces at McDowell."[16]

Colonel Jones, with the two companies of the Bath Cavalry and as many "Rangers" as were willing to go along, marched for Williamsville. Although the date of the incident is not clearly stated, it is believed that the troops arrived at Williamsville on May 7.

En route to Williamsville, Jones tried to learn from citizens the number of Federals, if any, in the town. The most plausible information indicated that the village was lightly held, that only three or four Yankees were present, and they were there only to nurse wounded comrades. On receipt of that report, Jones decided to enter the village, parole the wounded and their nurses and move on toward McDowell.

Colonel Jones and his command had not gone very far before they were approached by two tearful-eyed young ladies. They beseeched Jones not to enter Williamsville because it was full of Yankees eagerly awaiting the arrival of the Southern cavalry. The horsemen glanced about them. On a hill beyond the village they spotted a number of Yankees apparently in line of battle. Perched on the doorsteps were several bluecoats and visible behind a stone wall and a ledge of rocks were what looked like Yankee caps.

Believing himself "well nigh caught in a trap,"[17] Jones ordered his men to fall back. He was confident that at least 300 Federals were in town ready to trap the Bath Cavalry.

To Jones's subsequent chagrin, he learned that, instead of 300 Yankees in the town, there were only about 30, who were there to arrest "a feeble old man and his daughter-in-law, and carry them to McDowell to appear before General Milroy as witnesses in the trial of certain prisoners."[18]

When all the facts of the incident were brought to light, it developed that the Yankees in town were there primarily to find a horse and buggy to convey their prisoners to McDowell. And the Yankees on the hill beyond the town, Reverend Price explained, "were making tracks for headquarters, with all their might and had merely paused to see if they could tell how many of the 'secesh' were after them."[19] Price added that, inasmuch as both sides were retreating, nobody was hurt, "unless it was from running and becoming overheated."[20]

Lieutenant J. Q. Barnes of the 73rd Ohio recalled the incident at Williamsville in a totally different light. Writing on December 15, 1890, the officer remembered that a short while after Milroy's foraging train had been attacked near the village, he was ordered to return to the place with 28 men. His mission as to assemble citizens who had knowledge of the

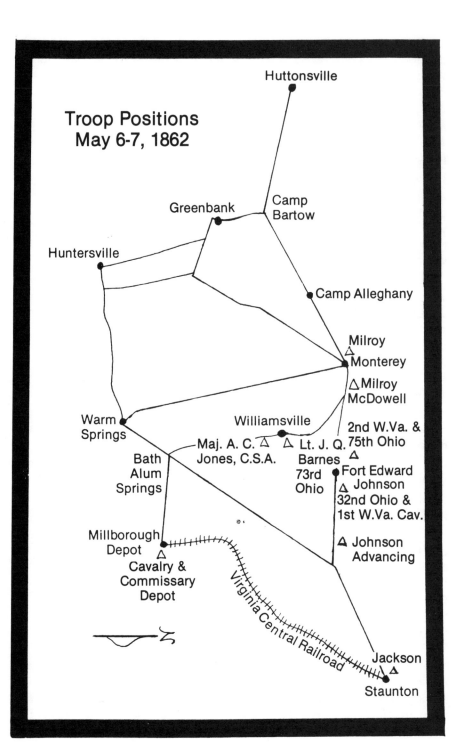

Troop Positions
May 6-7, 1862

Huttonsville

Camp
Bartow

Greenbank

Huntersville

Camp Alleghany

Milroy
Monterey

△Milroy
McDowell

Warm
Springs

Williamsville

2nd W.Va. &
75th Ohio

Maj. A. C. △ △ Lt. J. Q.
Jones, C.S.A. Barnes

Bath
Alum
Springs

73rd
Ohio

Fort Edward
△ Johnson
32nd Ohio &
1st W.Va. Cav.

Millborough
Depot

△ Johnson
Advancing

△
Cavalry &
Commissary
Depot

Virginia Central Railroad

Jackson
△
Staunton

bushwhacking incident. This was on either May 6 or 7.

According to Barnes, word of his approach leaked out and an ambush was prepared on his expected route of march. He avoided the trap, he said, by taking a different road. After the witnesses had been collected, Barnes visited Frank J. Esker, who was recovering at Williamsville from a serious wound received during the ambush of the wagon train. While speaking with Esker, the lieutenant was notified by a guard that Confederate cavalry was nearing the village. Immediately, he ordered his troops to fall in. They ran about 100 yards to the end of the main street. There they formed a line of battle and waited. Before long the Rebels appeared. What next happened, according to Barnes, was as follows:

> The boys stood calmly with orders not to fire until they came close enough to do good execution. Jimmy Ferguson stepped out about 3 paces to [the] front, drew a bead as deliberately as could be. I said 'Don't fire — let them get closer.' He said, 'Oh, how I would like to shoot that fellow.'[21]

When the Confederates realized that Barnes planned to stand and fight, they withdrew. The Yankees did likewise, moving to a hill near a mill. From there Barnes retreated to a place he identified as "Hard Scrabble." Here Barnes expected another engagement, but was "pleasantly disappointed" when it did not materialize.[22]

As Barnes's small detachment continued toward McDowell, Rebel horsemen threatened their progress, but were frightened away by approximately 200 Federal foragers. These foragers, in turn, were ordered back to McDowell because Milroy was being threatened by a Confederate force.

When Barnes returned to camp, he reported to Colonel Orlando Smith and inquired about a message he had sent by courier asking for help. Colonel Smith revealed that he had advised Milroy of Barnes's predicament and was told: "too bad, it's d----d bad, but I can't help it."[23]

In writing about the episode 28 years later, Barnes said he often wondered why his small group had been sent out "into the face of the enemy — 15 miles — when the evening before we had been notified to be ready to fight or retreat from McDowell."[24]

General Milroy's apparent lack of concern for the safety of Barnes's detachment was likely due to major activity on his front. Ordered by Fremont to fall back west of Shenandoah Mountain, Milroy maintained that Jackson's march from Staunton was nothing more than a feint to relieve pressure on Johnson. Milroy expressed his views to his superior:

> I shall not retire beyond this point, but in case of an attack by a superior force will await re-enforcements — Schenck's

and Blenker's force. I cannot give up the country now in our possession. Why cannot they [Schenck and Blenker] move up rapidly, and then push on vigorously together and clear the department before the May days are over? I may, in case of threatened attack, move on some 7 miles to Shaw's Ridge and make a stand there, if permission is granted. I will try and report to you from Staunton within forty-eight hours.[25]

General Milroy's last sentence defies understanding. He had received no orders to advance from McDowell and, even if he had, it certainly had to be clear to Milroy that he would require more than 48 hours to dispose of Johnson and Jackson.

In preparation for whatever lay ahead, Milroy made a number of dispositions during the first week of May. He ordered a large portion of the 3rd (West) Virginia, 32nd Ohio and 75th Ohio, together with a detachment of cavalry, to Shaw's Ridge and Shenandoah Mountain to protect his scouts and foragers. In another move, the 32nd Ohio and some cavalry crossed Shenandoah Mountain and camped at the eastern base. The 3rd (West) Virginia and 75th Ohio remained on Shaw's Fork on the western slope of the mountain.[26]

In Staunton, meanwhile, there was high expectation of impending battle. William Gregory was one who sensed an early clash of arms. The lieutenant of the 23rd Virginia who had only two days to live wrote on May 6:

What General Jackson intends doing now, I can't tell, but am of the impression that there is some heavy work ahead, as there has been great activity in military affairs here for the last two or three weeks. . . [27]

Some of the activity mentioned by Gregory was taking place as he wrote. Ordered to leave knapsacks, tents and other accoutrements behind, Johnson's troops commenced a march westward at noon on May 6. They camped that night at Dry Branch Gap on Big North Mountain. Earlier, when Jackson crossed the Blue Ridge and was believed on his way to Richmond, spirits fell in Johnson's command. They interpreted the move as a sign of abandonment of the Shenandoah Valley and the homes they had vowed to defend.

Now, however, the picture was changing dramatically.They were "elated with joy, when their faces were turned once more towards their homes."[28] With Jackson's Army of the Valley joining them, the men in Johnson's ranks rejoiced "in their holy duty of reclaiming their own homes."[29]

CHAPTER VI

May 7, 1862

The first confrontation of Jackson's renowned Valley Campaign was only one day off when Milroy, on May 7, made new deployments at McDowell. The 32nd Ohio and a cavalry company were assigned to Mason's Shanties on the east side of Shenandoah Mountain. Support units were posted on the western slope of the mountain. General Robert C. Schenck's division at this time was still nine miles south of Franklin. General Fremont arrived at Petersburg during the evening of the 7th, and the location of Blenker's division remained a mystery.[1]

Although the forces of Johnson and Jackson had begun their advance the day before, Milroy remained unaware of their proximity. In addition to the main force marching from Staunton, cavalry under Lieutenant Colonel Alexander C. Jones was approaching McDowell from the south to divert the Federals' attention from their chief threat on the Parkersburg Turnpike.

For a small number of Yankees, there was a more pressing matter in McDowell on May 7 than the threat of battle. This was a court martial convened by Lieutenant Norvel W. Truxal of the 2nd (West) Virginia Infantry to try the suspects in the Williamsville bushwhacking case. The court, which had met in the front room of a "public house" and had sentenced one man, accused of being the ringleader, to be shot,[2] when a messenger arrived with news that Jackson was nearing the village. Court was adjourned instantly and, as far as is known, the sentence was never carried out.[3]

General Edward Johnson's Army of the Northwest which led the march to McDowell numbered, 3,678 men, divided as follows:

FIRST BRIGADE
Colonel Z. T. Conner
May 6, 1862

12th Georgia Infantry	690
25th Virginia Infantry	546
31st Virginia Infantry	589
Captain Charles I. Raine's Battery	74
Total	1,899

SECOND BRIGADE
Colonel W. C. Scott
May 5, 1862

44th Virginia Infantry 405
52nd Virginia Infantry 693
58th Virginia Infantry 487
Captain John A. M. Lusk's Battery 95
Captain William H. Rice's Battery 99
  Total 1,779
  GRAND TOTAL .... 3,678[4]

Of this force, less than 3,400 were engaged in the battle of McDowell. Of course the artillery was not engaged, and there were a number of men detached from the 25th Virginia Infantry.

The Valley Army consisted of:

FIRST BRIGADE
Brigadier General C. S. Winder

2nd Virginia Infantry 758
4th Virginia Infantry 840
5th Virginia Infantry 902
27th Virginia Infantry 418
33rd Virginia Infantry 763
  Total 3,681

SECOND BRIGADE
Colonel J. A. Campbell

1st Virginia Infantry, PACS 366
21st Virginia Infantry............................... 600
42nd Virginia Infantry 750
48th Virginia Infantry 800
  Total 2,516

THIRD BRIGADE
Brigadier General William B. Taliaferro

10th Virginia Infantry 700
23rd Virginia Infantry 600
37th Virginia Infantry 900
  Total 2,200
  GRAND TOTAL .... 8,577[5]

These figures do not include the V.M.I. Cadets, Ashby's cavalry and the batteries of Edward Marye, James Waters, Lindsay Shumaker, Joseph Carpenter and William T. Poague. With these commands added to it, the Valley Army would probably be over 9,500 strong. Of this force, only about

44

4,700 were engaged in the actual fighting at McDowell. The combined strength of Jackson's and Johnson's armies came to little over 13,000, of which approximately 8,100 were actually engaged in the Battle of McDowell.

The Confederate movement toward McDowell was initiated on May 6 by the brigades of Edward Johnson. The Valley Army stepped out on May 7, with William Taliaferro's Third Brigade in the van, followed by John Campbell's Second Brigade and Charles S. Winder's First (Stonewall) Brigade. About 800 members of Ashby's cavalry guarded the rear, camping that night near Buffalo Gap.[6]

The V.M.I. Cadets marched with the Stonewall Brigade under the Institute Superintendent Frances H. Smith. In the words of one historian: "The spruce equipments and exact drill of these youths, as they stepped out full of enthusiasm to take their first actual look upon the horrid visage of war. . . formed a strong contrast with the war-worn and nonchalant veterans who composed the army.[7]

To many of the "war-torn and nonchalant veterans," the country through which they were tramping was familiar scenery. They had viewed it during Robert E. Lee's ill-fated Western Virginia Campaign of the previous year.

General Johnson broke camp on North Mountain early on May 7. When the head of his column reached the junction of the Turnpike and the Harrisonburg-Warm Springs road it was fired on by Captain Shuman's (1st West Virginia) Cavalry. Quickly, Johnson ordered the 31st Virginia to the front to reinforce the 52nd Virginia, but by the time the men arrived, they saw only dead horses and riders.

While this skirmish was underway, the 58th Virginia was ordered to a ridge on the right of the Turnpike. From that elevation, the infantrymen gazed down upon enemy cavalrymen riding leisurely to and fro. The column moved on until it neared Mason's Shanties, from where a company was sent on ahead. Charles C. Wight described what happened next: "In a few minutes we hear the clatter of horses feet and then a volley from the detached company. We instantly hurry on, but the enemy has escaped, leaving several dead horses and two prisoners in the hands of our comrades. A few minutes more and we would doubtless have captured this entire squadron of cavalry."[8]

The preliminaries to the Battle of McDowell were now drawing rapidly to a close. General Milroy and his cohorts had been unaware that Jackson was heading their way until the morning of May 7. As the 32nd Ohio was eating breakfast in their camp at Rodgers' Toll House, and awaiting the return of the regimental wagons so forage could be removed and their tents thrown in, a rider, ". . . bare-headed and dusty, with saber in hand, dashed through the camp at the utmost speed . . . shouting as he flew by, 'The rebels are coming!' "[9] Following close behind rode other cavalrymen who repeated the warning.

Inasmuch as there had been no hint of a threat from pickets, a strong suspicion existed that there were only bushwhackers to the east. Just to be on the safe side, several companies of the 32nd Ohio were sent in that direction, while the remainder of the men prepared to move one way or the other. It was indeed true. Unmistakably, the Rebels were approaching. The 32nd Ohio fell back to the top of Shenandoah Mountain,[10] leaving behind huge quantities of equipment and personal baggage. Exactly how many casualties resulted from this engagement between the Federal advance guard and the Confederate skirmishers is difficult to determine. One source reported the Yankees lost two killed and as many taken prisoner. Another account lists three killed and one captured. Still a third report states that six Federals were wounded. The 32nd Ohio, which had been on picket duty, lost about 20 prisoners.[11] The regimental history, however, insists that the pickets escaped into the mountains. There is no record of any Confederate casualties.

Once it was established that the enemy was in their front, Milroy and his subordinates took precipitate action. The 73rd Ohio and a battery were rushed to the support of the 75th Ohio and the 2nd (West) Virginia. About noon the force was hurried forward under the immediate command of General Milroy. A few miles from McDowell the support force met the retreating 75th Ohio. Together, the regiments hastened on. The column climbed Shaw's Ridge. Below were the graycoats advancing toward McDowell.[12]

After forcing the Federals to abandon their position on the east side of Shenandoah Mountain, the Confederates helped themselves to the abandoned equipment and searched the personal baggage left behind. Among the items captured were the sutler stores belonging to Sid Stocking. These stores, according to the regimental history of the 32nd Ohio "constituted no unimportant part of the capture."[13]

By this time Jackson had ridden to the head of the column. He suspected that the Federals would occupy the abandoned Confederate fortifications on the crest of the mountain and resist the progress of his army. As a precaution, Jackson ordered two detachments of skirmishers to advance up the mountain along the spurs on either side of the road. Jed Hotchkiss led the skirmishers on the right, while Colonel Williamson led those on the left.[14] After a difficult climb, Hotchkiss reached the crest of the mountain and moved toward Fort Johnson. There he found that the Federals had not halted at the top of the mountain, but were retiring across Shaw's Ridge. From that point, Hotchkiss signaled the way was clear, and Johnson's army advanced.

After reaching the summit of the mountain, the Confederates waited until their artillery could be brought up to cover their further advance. Once the artillery was in position, the 31st Virginia led the way down the mountain.

At Shaw's Fork, a stream running between Shenandoah Mountain and Shaw's Ridge, the Southerners came under fire from Captain Hyman's Battery of 12-pounders.

At the same time the Unionist spotted a Rebel detachment on their right about two miles away. General Milroy called for Company B, of the 32nd Ohio and instructed the captain, "If you find them, pitch into them; give them h--l. Make them think they are flanked."[15]

From all indications, Milroy did not wait for the captain's report of the expedition. The general wrote: ". . . being prohibited by Fremont to bring a general engagement, I thought it prudent to fall back to McDowell. . ."[16]

Withdrawal did not diminish Milroy's determination to fight. In the expectation that Johnson would attack his front while Jackson struck his left from North River Gap, Milroy declared he "would not yield a foot to treason, and so we must fight."[17]

William H. Hull was a resident of Pocahontas County and first sergeant of Company G, 31st Virginia. Years later he wrote:

> The men of our regiment were in high glee on account of traveling in the direction of our homes. They were marching at quick step, cheering and joking in fine style when a little puff of smoke was seen on Shaw's Ridge and at the same instant a shell went whistling over our heads, followed in quick succession by several others, some of which struck almost in our ranks on the hard road bed and rocheted to the rear. We were not slow in surrendering our rights in the public highway.[18]

Although nine shells were said to have been lobbed into the Confederate column,[19] the one described by Hull was enough to send the graycoats scampering for the protection of the trees that bordered the Turnpike.

With the sun sinking behind the ridges, Johnson called a halt to the day's action. Part of his command went into bivouac at the Marshall Toll Gate on Shaw's Fork. It was a night that none of the men would soon forget. First came an order to remain in line and stay quiet, while prohibiting campfires. Then the temperature plunged and frost covered the camp with a mantle of white. According to Sergeant Hull, "there was a good deal of shivering and chattering of teeth and very little sleeping."[20]

While the men sought bodily comfort and awaited the dawn of a new day, a field hospital was established on Shaw's Fork to care for the wounded in the forcoming engagement.[21] Generals Jackson and Johnson set up their headquarters at William Rodger's Toll Gate, at which had been the Yankees' encampment. The distance from this point to the rear of Confederate line was probably ten miles.[22]

On May 7, the ever-vigilant Jackson ordered a scouting party to determine the strength of that portion of Fremont's army that was believed to be on its way to reinforce Milroy. The detachment, composed of soldiers from Pendleton County and commanded by Captain E. W. Boggs of the 25th Virginia,[23] started on its assignment on May 7. The following day, Boggs was on Evick Ridge east of Franklin.

As the roar of cannon rumbled in the distance at McDowell, Boggs studied the town before him. Foremost in his thoughts was a raid on the lightly-held village and capture of valuable stores. The captain dismissed this notion when Yankee cavalry appeared on the streets below. Despite the presence of the horsemen, some of Boggs's men slipped into Franklin and obtained important information from a Southern sympathizer.

The next day, [May 9], as Jackson and Johnson began the pursuit of the beaten enemy at McDowell, the scouting party was at Wilson Hole near the village of Ruddle. After dark the Rebels cut the telegraph line at several points north of Franklin and then stretched the wire across the road at a height designed to unseat a horseman riding into it.

The Confederates retired into the darkness and waited. Before long their mischief was rewarded. Yankee cavalrymen, curious about the break in the telegraph, galloped swiftly into the trap and were knocked from their saddles. Though bruised, they escaped without serious consequences.[24]

Before rejoining their comrades, Boggs's men visited the home of Ambrose Meadows. While resting and having a bite to eat, the scouts were surprised by the approach of two Yankees. One of them they killed, the second was wounded. This attack brought disastrous reprisals on Ambrose Meadows, who was later killed by Federal troops.[25]

As the day wore on, General Milroy became jittery as he made ready for the impending clash with the Valley Army at McDowell. On May 7 he sent a dispatch to General Schenck:

"Enemy pressing us. Our forces thus far engaged are parts of three regiments. Must have aid. Have reason to believe that part of the enemy are coming up North River Gap, to prevent junction of your forces with mine; inform Fremont. Cannot Blenker's force make a forced march, relieve you and myself? Cannot you join me? Ask Fremont to have Banks press on in the rear of Jackson."[26]

In mid-afternoon Schenck advised Fremont that he would "hasten on to Milroy's support."[27] General Milroy also was informed that Schenck was on his way. In response to that piece of intelligence, Milroy suggested that Schenck come by way of Monterey and leave his most fatigued companies at that place. General Milroy recommended further that the wearied companies replace those of the 2nd (West) Virginia, which could then accompany Schecnk to McDowell. General Milroy felt that the enemy "will almost be certain to attack me at daylight."[28]

In yielding ground to the Confederates, Milroy created an undercurrent of discontent among some officers, particularly those who "expected to go right forward to Richmond, because of this retrograde movement, more especially because two mountain passes were given up that could have been held against almost any force."[29]

Private John S. Sosman was an eye witness to Federal preparations on the eve of the battle. From his hospital bed in the Presbyterian Church, he wrote in his diary:

> Everything is in a great "hubbub" out doors. The artillery is all gone out and is planted on a hill commanding the approach to the town from the North-east from which direction the rebels are reported to be marching on us. Cavalrymen can bee seen riding furiously in all directions carrying orders to and fro.[30]

General Milroy's men slept on their arms that night, speculating on what the morrow might bring.

CHAPTER VII

May 8, 1862 - Phase I.

When Osborn Wilson awoke on the morning of May 8, there was frost on the ground in all directions. Later in the day the 29-year-old sergeant of the 31st Virginia confided to his diary: "...indications were that all would be warm enough in more ways than one ere nightfall."[1]

The days march toward McDowell started at an early hour with the 52nd Virginia at the head of the column. During the morning two companies of Turner Ashby's cavalry, which had been bringing up the rear, joined the advance.[2]

The Confederates crossed Shaw's Ridge and descended into the Cow Pasture River Valley. The Bull Pasture Mountain loomed just ahead. As the men wound their way toward the crest, Jed Hotchkiss preceded them. At each turn of the road, Hotchkiss turned and waved his handkerchief if it was safe to march on, thereby allowing the column to advance more rapidly than would have been possible otherwise. Yankee cavalry pickets yielded the mountain top without a contest.[3] Joseph Snider, a private in the 31st Virginia, disclosed that shots were exchanged on the summit but nothing more.[4]

From the crest of Bull Pasture Mountain, Johnson's Army of the Northwest could glance to the rear. Across the valley they could see the "dark serpentine lines" of Jackson's troops descending Shenandoah Mountain.[5]

Reveille sounded in the Federal camp at 2:30 a.m. on May 8. By 4 o'clock breakfast was eaten, the sick were moved a mile to the rear and the battle line was established for an expected attack at daybreak. The 73rd Ohio was posted on the extreme right and a portion of the 3rd (West) Virginia on Hull's Hill on the opposite flank. From there the Yankees could see the enemy but were too far away to deliver an effective fire. Between the two flanks were the 75th Ohio, 32nd Ohio, 25th Ohio and the remainder of the 3rd (West) Virginia. Three companies of the 1st (West) Virginia Cavalry were stationed on the road leading to Doe Hill near McDowell. Captain Henry Hyman's battery was located on high ground in rear of the Presbyterian Church. Close by was the greater portion of the 2nd (West) Virginia Infantry.[6]

Other guns were positioned on a ridge west of McDowell along the road to Monterey. A map by Hotchkiss shows four guns at this site. Overall, Hotchkiss indicated nine pieces of artillery behind the church.[7] It

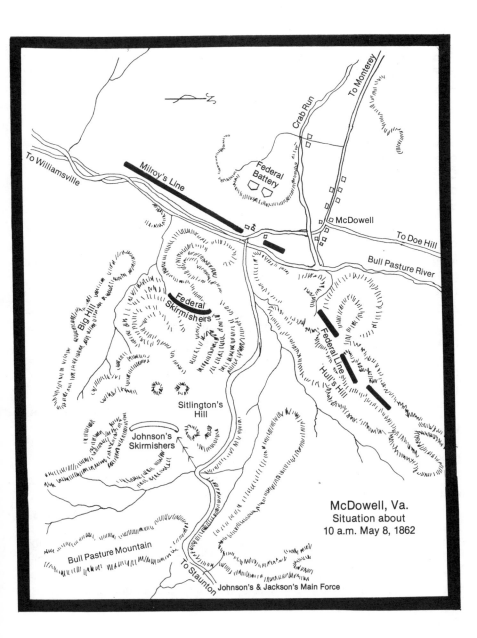

To Williamsville

To Monterey

Crab Run

Milroy's Line

Federal Battery

McDowell

To Doe Hill

Bull Pasture River

Big Hill

Federal Skirmishers

Federal Line

Hull's Hill

Sitlington's Hill

Johnson's Skirmishers

McDowell, Va.
Situation about
10 a.m. May 8, 1862

Bull Pasture Mountain

To Staunton

Johnson's & Jackson's Main Force

is entirely possible that there were several other guns positioned at another point.

General Milroy's command consisted of the following infantry regiments: 2nd and 3rd (West) Virginia, 25th Ohio (nine companies), 32nd Ohio (nine companies, 73rd Ohio and 75th Ohio (seven companies). General Milroy also had with him the 1st (1st) Virginia Cavalry, (Companies C, E and L), Battery I, 1st Ohio Light Artillery, Captain Henry F. Hyman; Battery G, 1st (West) Virginia Light Artillery and the 12th Ohio Independent Battery, Captain Aaron C. Johnson.[8]

In the engagement that was due to commence in mid-afternoon, four of Milroy's infantry regiments participated. Together with their numerical strength, they were the 25th Ohio (469 men), 32nd Ohio (416 men), 75th Ohio (444 men), and 3rd (West) Virginia (439 men). Excluding artillery, cavalry, scouts and skirmishers, Milroy's strength did not exceed 1,768 men.

At the same time that Milroy was forming his line of defense, the brigade of General Robert C. Schenck was about five miles from Monterey. Thirteen miles lay between him and Milroy, but Schenck reported to John C. Fremont that he hoped his "little force may yet be in time to do something."[9]

General Schenck's command consisted of the 1st Battalion Connecticut Cavalry (250 men), 5th (West) Virginia Infantry, 55th Ohio Infantry (seven companies), 82nd Ohio Infantry, Battery K, 1st Ohio Light Artillery, Captain William L. DeBeck, and the 3rd Regiment, Potomac Home Guards at Moorefield.[10] General Schenck's command numbered fewer than 2,000 men.[11]

When Milroy was not attacked at daybreak as he had expected, the general ordered cavalry toward North River Gap in an effort to find Jackson's column. The horsemen rode 15 miles before returning and reporting they had seen nothing of the enemy.

The Rebels had resumed their march at an early hour and about 10 o'clock were halted by General Edward Johnson on the crest of Bull Pasture Mountain. From there the general, some staff officers and thirty members of the 52nd Virginia reconnoitered the countryside. In checking the terrain, Johnson found a path to the top of Sitlington's Hill. By leaving the Staunton-Parkersburg Turnpike at a sharp angle on the left, and following a steep, boulder-strewn ravine, Johnson determined that it was possible to attain the high table land, from which the Federal camp was plainly visible.

When Jackson arrived on Bull Pasture Mountain, he beckoned to Jed Hotchkiss, who had conducted a school in the area and was familiar with the geographical features of it. The two proceeded to a ledge of rocks on the right of the road. For a long time they surveyed the valley below and studied Milroy's line. When they caught up with Johnson some time later, "Old Alleghany" was moving skirmishers to the top of Sitlington's Hill. This eminence at the top was:

> ...broad but was rugged and had many sharp ridges and ravines on its surface. In front of it, a smooth slope dropped down sharply to the Bull Pasture River, about 500 feet below... a ridge that ran North and South, and at right angles to the turnpike. It had a depression in it a little to the northern side of the center of the ridge. At the extreme northern end of the ridge, beyond another small depression, was a small wooded knoll. This ridge does not go straight north and south but is a ridge of three different hills (the before mentioned two depressions separating them) forming an obtuse angle. From the apex of this angle another ridge runs southwest to a ravine that goes down to the Bull Pasture River. It is a fairly steep climb coming from the west up to the obtuse angled Sitlington's Ridge, especially on its center and southern end. There is a deep depression between the northwest running and the southwest running ridges, mentioned above. Thus you have a picture somewhat like two angles coming together at their apexes. This hill is constantly running down hill from the obtuse angled ridge down to its apex and then further down along the arms of the lower angle. Behind the upper ridge there is a big sinkhole and then woods behind that.[12]

In most respects, Ed Johnson was satisfied with the Confederates' position on Sitlington's Hill. Because the summit was in the shape of a curve, with the convexity toward the enemy, Johnson's center was open to fire from several sides. On the flanks, the curve rose into shaley spines and was a good defensive position.[13]

While moving about on the crest of the hill, the Rebels attracted the attention of the Yankees in the valley below. Without delay, Milroy ordered three companies of the 73rd Ohio (Major Long) and Captain Latham's Company of the 2nd (West) Virginia to advance as skirmishers.

At the same time the general directed the artillery to open fire on the graycoats, who were about one and three-quarter miles away. The gunners elevated their cannon as much as possible. When they failed to get the range in that manner, they dropped the trails of the guns into trenches in an effort to attain greater elevation. That, too, was unsuccessful. The whole effort, according to Frank S. Reader of the 2nd (West) Virginia, was made primarily "to ascertain their numbers. . ."[14]

The Federal skirmishers advanced up the hill and opened fire on the

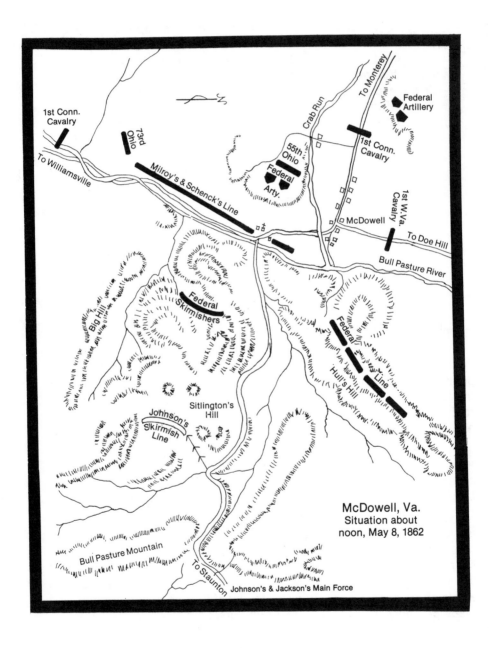

1st Conn.
Cavalry

73rd Ohio

To Williamsville

Milroy's & Schenck's Line

To Monterey

Crab Run

Federal
Artillery

1st Conn.
Cavalry

55th Ohio

Federal
Arty.

McDowell

1st W.Va.
Cavalry

To Doe Hill

Bull Pasture River

Federal
Skirmishers

Big Hill

Federal Line

Hull's Hill

Sitlington's Hill

Johnson's
Skirmish
Line

McDowell, Va.
Situation about
noon, May 8, 1862

Bull Pasture Mountain

To Staunton

Johnson's & Jackson's Main Force

detachment of the 52nd Virginia Infantry which had accompanied General Johnson. The Confederates returned their fire, and drove the Federals back.[15]

In order to secure the Rebel position on Sitlington's Hill, Johnson's army was sent to him. The 52nd Virginia was the first Southern regiment to reach the field. It was positioned on the far left, from where it repulsed the first attack of Federal skirmishers.

The 12th Georgia was the next unit to arrive on the field. It was positioned on the crest and formed the center of Johnson's line, the key to the field. When the 58th arrived, it was ordered to the left to act as support for the 52nd. Charles C. Wight described the position of the 58th:

> We are posted along the crest of this hill, and one company is sent to occupy the summit of another knoll near the village and the enemy. We watch this company as it approaches this point, for we think it probable that we will all follow them, if the coast is clear; just as the advance file of the men [peered] over the ridge the whole company recoiled and began a precipitate retreat to our line and at the same moment the eminence glittered with the guns of the Federal troops who raised a shout and open fire on the retiring company. We are all within full range and their bullets whistle about us. As soon as the men who had been thrown in advance reach our line we return the fire. More of the enemy now make their appearance from the valley below and they seem resolved to drive us from the hill. A battery opens on us from a hill near the village, but our [position] is so high that the balls pass over us without doing much harm.[16]

The 44th Virginia arrived next. It was placed on the right of the line, its right resting on a ravine and its left next to the 12th Georgia. To prevent a possible Federal advance from McDowell and a charge up the ravine to the rear of the Confederates, Jackson positioned the 31st Virginia on the road a little before the ravine. Very likely there was cavalry in the same area.[17]

The precise location of the 25th Virginia at this time is unclear. Colonel George H. Smith insisted that his regiment was posted on the extreme right. General Jackson reported that the regiment was not brought into action until later. A third account maintains that the 25th Virginia was held in reserve because its ranks had been thinned by details from it.[18]

Before being ordered into position on the turnpike, the 31st Virginia had been resting near the top of Bull Pasture Mountain. According to Sergeant Osborn Wilson, a section of artillery was ordered to take position on Sitlington's Hill, but was unable to find a route to the top. According to the history of the 1st Rockbridge Artillery, the "Stonewall Battery" had been ordered into the fight, but could not be brought into position, and returned to the Cow Pasture River Valley.[19]

Following the repulse of the Federal skirmishers, artillery opened on the Rebels atop Sitlington's Hill. John S. Robson of the 52nd Virginia recorded that:

[the Yankees] opened on us with their artillery a rapid and incessant fire of case shot and shell, but 'us boys' laid low among the rocks and trees, which afforded us ample protection, and also the angle of elevation and their guns being so great, no damage, except to the timber, resulted from this cannonade.[20]

It was approximately 10:30 a.m. when Schenck's brigade arrived at McDowell. By leaving his baggage train behind "in my last camp. . . fourteen miles from McDowell," the prewar lawyer in Dayton, O. covered "thirty-four miles in twenty-three hours." Said Milroy, the arrival was "just in time."[21]

Informing Fremont of his arrival, Schecnk noted "All seems prepared for receiving them [the Confederates] as warmly as inferior numbers will admit. . . .Where is General Banks at this juncture? Where is Blenker's division?"[22]

General Banks, on May 8, was at New Market, pursuant to orders to withdraw from Harrisonburg and take position at Strasburg. From all indications this bit of intelligence had not been transmitted to either Schenck or Milroy. As for Blenker, the one-time German revolutionary was far from the scene of the impending battle. He was believed to be near Romney in Hampshire County.

Although Schecnk was Milroy's superior, he deferred command of their combined forces to the junior officer who was more familiar with what had already taken place. After looking over the situation at McDowell, Schenck concluded that Milroy's position could not be defended, therefore they would follow Fremont's orders and withdraw to Franklin. This could not be done, however, in broad daylight or without determining the actual strength of the Rebels.

Deployment of Schenck's brigade found the 55th Ohio placed in rear of Hyman's Battery and the 82nd Ohio fused into Milroy's line.[23] The 5th (West) Virginia was assigned to Milroy's left between the Presbyterian Church and Hyman's Battery. Captain DeBeck's Battery was in close proximity to Hyman's although its exact position is not expressly indicated. The 1st Battalion Connecticut Cavalry was divided into two sections. The first was placed on the turnpike west of McDowell, the other on the road south of McDowell toward Williamsville and below the 73rd Ohio.[24]

After a full study of the terrain and deployments, Jackson decided against placing artillery on Sitlington's Hill for two reasons. First, if he bombarded the Federals in McDowell, they would escape with scant damage. Second, if he succeeded in dragging his guns across the rugged terrain and was subsequently forced to retreat, the descent was too steep for a quick withdrawal of the guns.

Instead, "Old Jack" concluded to move his artillery to Milroy's rear. To find a road for this operation, the general turned to his proven factotum, Jed Hotchkiss. Once such a route was discovered, it was Hotchkiss's responsibility to have the artillery in position by 3 a.m. on May 9.

Any thought of a frontal assault on Milroy was dismissed by Jackson because of the character of the land. It was not only extremely rugged, but there also was the rain-swollen Bull Pasture River to cross. An attack by the road was impracticable, too. As soon as his men came into view of the Yankees they would invite a murderous fire.

After weighing all the factors, Jackson concluded that there would be no major action in the remaining hours of that Thursday. Accordingly, he dismissed most of his staff and directed them to return to his headquarters at John Wilson's Hotel on the eastern base of Bull Pasture Mountain. He remained at the eastern base on Sitlington's Hill overseeing Johnson's troops.[25]

Desultory firing continued until mid-afternoon with little consequence other than to enable Milroy to ascertain the strength of his adversaries. During the skirmishing the Northern commander ordered a detachment from Company G, 75th Ohio to join his line of skirmishers.[26]

CHAPTER VIII
The Battle of McDowell
May 8, 1862 - Phase II

As Federal officers speculated on the battle strategy of their Confederate counterparts, a company captain, George R. Latham, informed General Robert H. Milroy that the Rebels were in the process of planting a battery on Sitlington's Hill. What gave Latham such an impression is not known. He may have assumed that since the enemy was building up its strength that placing artillery on the hill was a natural thing to do.

The false rumor spurred Milroy into action. Artillery on Sitlington's Hill would place the Federals at the mercy of their enemy. General Milroy saw at that instant that "...he must at once take the aggressive or abandon the field. His restless nature and love of conflict prevailing. . ."[1]

General Milroy conferred with Robert C. Schenck. Waiting for reinforcements was out of the question since there were no other Union troops within 60 miles. That left only one option. They decided to "deliver a blow, if we could, and then retire from his [Jackson's] front before he had recovered from the surprise. . ."[2]

As a result, General Milroy made a reconnaissance in force to learn the strength and position of the enemy. The operation was so successful that Schenck reported: "No officer could have carried it out more effectively than did General Milroy."[3]

E. Z. Hays, writing in his history of the 32nd Ohio, described the situation:

> It was now determined to not only risk an engagement, but to attack the enemy in a very strong position chosen by himself on the top of Bull Pasture Mountain [Sitlington's Hill] — a position almost impregnable if defended with reasonable skill and courage. It was a position that should not have been attacked at all, unless the attacking force so greatly outnumbered the defenders as that a considerable body could have been detached for the purpose of gaining the enemy's flank or rear. The attack was delivered squarely in the enemy's face, but most forcibly upon his right flank.[4]

The hour that the assault began varies from one source to another. One historian gives the time as 3:30 p.m.; a second records it as late as 6:15. In all probability, the attack was launched between 4 and 5 o'clock. About 4:30 p.m., Milroy ordered his artillerist to increase their rate of fire.[5]

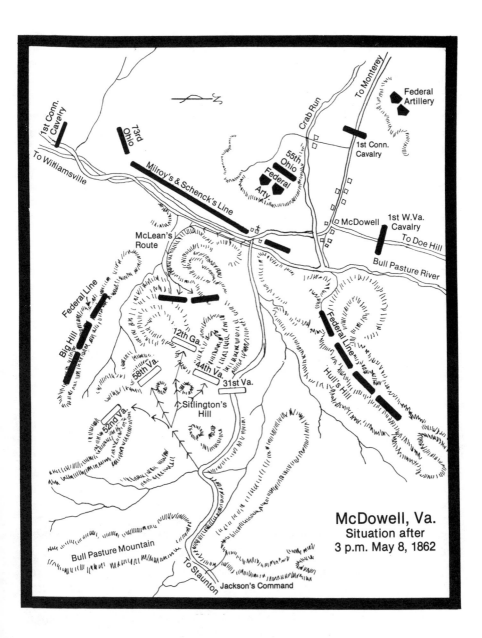

McDowell, Va.
Situation after
3 p.m. May 8, 1862

1st Conn. Cavalry

73rd Ohio

To Williamsville

Milroy's & Schenck's Line

McLean's Route

Federal Line

Big Hill

12th Ga.

58th Va.

44th Va.

31st Va.

Sitlington's Hill

52nd Va.

Bull Pasture Mountain

To Staunton

Jackson's Command

Crab Run

To Monterey

Federal Artillery

55th Ohio

Federal Arty.

1st Conn. Cavalry

McDowell

1st W.Va. Cavalry

To Doe Hill

Bull Pasture River

Federal Line

Hull's Hill

Under cover of the accelerated but ineffective fire, the 25th and 75th Ohio regiments, numbering just over 900 men, were ordered to attack the Confederate position on Sitlington's Hill where Edward Johnson was studying the situation on the right of his line.[6]

Colonel N. C. McLean, commanding the attack force, led the two regiments across the Bull Pasture River, then along a road that paralleled the river for several hundred yards. The skirmishers, who had been engaged since morning, were now pulled back and took a position near the artillery.

From the river road, McLean turned to the left and marched through a ravine leading to the Confederate front. Nearly a mile of woodland separated McLean and the open ground where the Rebels lay in wait for him.

Shortly after entering the ravine, McLean directed Lieutenant Colonel W. P. Richardson of the 25th Ohio, which was in the lead, to send two companies to the forefront to serve as skirmishers. In quick succession, McLean also ordered Richardson to support the skirmishers with the remainder of his regiment in line of battle.[7]

Progress through the ravine was agonizingly slow and tedious. Boulders, trees and rugged terrain took a heavy toll of the men and by the time they had proceeded two-thirds of the way, they were in a state of near exhaustion.[8]

As they advanced into open ground the Federals were confronted by a Confederate force several times the size of their own. They were met by a devastating shower of lead but, reported McLean, "Under the most heavy and galling fire from a well sheltered enemy, and without protection themselves, they steadily advanced up the precipitous ascent, firing and loading with great coolness. . ."[9]

Suddenly, the Federals charged. Hand-to-hand combat ensued and the Confederates were driven into a basin higher up the hill. The 12th Georgia, however, did not retreat entirely. When Colonel Z. T. Conner persuaded one wing of the regiment to retire, the opposite wing would rush forward until Conner ordered it to the rear, whereupon the other wing would return to its original position. Later a Georgian was asked why they had not sought the protection of the ridge. Bluntly, he replied, "We did not come all this way to Virginia to run before the Yankees."[10] The Georgians were brave, but foolish, and it cost them dearly.

While the battle was in its early stages, Jackson was on the turnpike. Telescope in hand, he gazed intently as the armies surged back and forth. Because he had a clear view of the right flank that was invisible to Johnson, "Old Jack" relayed orders to the various regiments through Lieutenant Hugh H. Lee, his chief of ordnance.[11]

After driving back the advance units of Johnson's army, McLean assailed the main Confederate line. This was W. C. Scott's Second Brigade consisting of the 52nd, 58th and 44th Virginia. The 12th Georgia was in front of Scott's line.

On orders from Johnson, Scott spaced his men along the crest of the hill. They were placed in pairs about five paces apart, leaving only a wooded hill on the right uncovered.

Only a brief time elapsed after the deployment before the 25th Ohio appeared on Scott's left flank. To meet the threat, the colonel sent out two companies of skirmishers to meet one company under McLean. The Confederates advanced, fired a single volley and fell back.

The tempo now accelerated. Colonel Scott ordered the front rank of his right to fire, then fall back several steps, lie down and reload. Then the entire process was to be repeated.[12]

After several rounds had been fired in this fashion, Scott detected some irregulatories in his ranks. Some men were falling back too far before reloading; others were lying prone and doing absolutely nothing. Colonel Scott, a prewar lawyer in Powhatan County, tried oral persuasion to arouse his men. It did no good. He tried threats. Again no results. At wit's end, the 53-year-old officer resorted to drastic measures. He rode his horse back and forth across the prostrate figures. The recalcitrants understood that message and rejoined the battle.

As the severity of fire intensified, Scott pulled the 44th Virginia out of line and repositioned it in a depression 30 yards behind the 58th Virginia. He gave two reasons for this move. First, the 44th was vulnerable to enemy fire, while being unable to inflict heavy damage on the Yankees. Second, if the 58th was forced to fall back, the 44th was there to serve as a support unit.[13] The rank and file of the 44th Virginia, however, had other ideas. As soon as the colonel's back was turned, they rushed back to the line, joining the 58th Virginia and possibly the 12th Georgia.

When Scott ordered the withdrawal of the 44th Virginia, he was unaware of General Edward Johnson's position on the field, and that execution of his order would expose the general to grave danger, perhaps even to capture. Fortunately for "Old Alleghany," Captain Edward M. Alfriend of the Richmond Zouaves perceived the peril. Instead of obeying the withdrawal order, Alfriend and his men charged the enemy and removed the general from harm's way.[14]

Following their initial success against the Confederates, McLean's two regiments held their ground for 90 minutes without assistance. The colonel praised the 25th and 75th Ohio for their commendable work, saying they ". . . worked together with great coolness and the men seemed only to be anxious to get steady aim when firing their pieces, without a thought of retiring."[15]

A reporter for the *Cincinnati Commercial* heaped bouquets on McLean's command, writing:

> Where the fight was the hottest and the men seemed to waver, there you would see Colonel McLean and Major [Robert] Reiley, cheering their men, and by their own daring and coolness inspiring confidence and courage in the men. They say the Major actually became excited, and got to making stump speeches to his boys, telling them to 'wipe out the stain that had fallen upon the name of Ohio on other fields.'[16]

In the words of one historian, McLean's attack ". . . was most daring and evidently impressed the enemy (as was, perhaps, intended) that we were ready and able to dispute their further advance."[17]

The position now occupied by the Confederates was an admirable one. They were able to fire on the Federals, while exposing only their heads. They would then duck down behind the ridge line and reload. While the Confederates were in a good position, they were silhouetted against the evening sky and made good targets. The Federals, on the other hand, were masked by the shadows cast by the setting sun.

Colonel McLean's lodgement on Sitlington's Hill exceeded Milroy's expectations. Anticipating an early retirement from the field, the general had failed to reinforce the colonel. Now, however, with the Union position secure, Milroy changed his mind. Three regiments, the 32nd and 82nd Ohio and the 3rd (West) Virginia, were ordered to try to turn the Confederates right. As they started forward a shout rang out: "Men, remember that you are from Ohio!" It came from General Robert C. Schenck, whose father had founded the Ohio River town of Franklin. Alfred E. Lee, in his history of the battle, asserted, "We did not forget it."[18]

Crossing the Bull Pasture River, the two Ohio regiments marched along the turnpike until they reached a long, wooded ravine on their right. They entered the ravine and eventually emerged on the right flank of the Confederates.

Alfred E. Lee's account of the battle, written in 1886, varies slightly from the official report. Lee maintained that the 82nd initially climbed Hull's Hill with one piece of artillery. After reaching the summit, the colonel reconsidered the move. He ordered his men off the ridge, across the turnpike and up Sitlington's Hill.[19]

While these infantrymen were moving into position, Milroy ordered a battery of six-pounders onto Hull's Hill. One report indicates that only one gun was involved in this operation, a second account insists it was an entire section while a third contends it was a battery. General Milroy himself gave conflicting reports. In his official account the general stated ".....a 6-pounder, of Johnson's battery, under the command of Lieutenant Powers, was with the greatest difficulty placed in position on the mountain on the left of the turnpike. . ."[20] In a letter to his wife, Milroy noted ". . .and by the most incredible exertions got two pieces of artillery up on a mountain as high as the ridge on which the rebels were."[21]

Regardless of the number of guns, the artillery rendered effective support to the infantry climbing Sitlington's Hill. When the Federal troops neared the Confederate line, Lieutenant Powers, who was in charge of the guns withheld his fire so as not to endanger the Yankee infantry.[22]

As evening drew near, General Milroy ordered additional artillery into action. The general ordered two 12-pounders of Captain Johnson's 12th Ohio (Independent) Battery forward, however, the two guns did not reach their position until after twilight, and by then it was too late.

Under cover of woods, the 32nd and 82nd Ohio advanced undetected to a point near the crest of the middle ridge of Sitlington's Hill. From there they delivered a crushing bayonet charge on the right of Johnson's line. The Confederates broke, then countercharged, only to fall back. A second countercharge, this time with reinforcements, regained some of the lost ground.

One member of the 82nd Ohio disclosed that the Rebels had built temporary breastworks out of trees and brush. As the battle progressed and the dead lay thick on the ground, it was alleged that the Southerners used the corpses as part of the works.[23]

Meanwhile, the 3rd (West) Virginia, which had remained on the turnpike while the two Ohio regiments struggled up the ravine, was engaged in a vigorous fight of its own against the 31st Virginia. The Rebels were stationed on the side of the hill, from where some riflemen slipped around to the Yankees' rear. Attacked thus from two directions, the (West) Virginians fired first at the troops in their front, reloaded, then turned and fired at those in their rear.

Not long after these two regiments faced off against each other, the 31st Virginia received orders to move up Sitlington's Hill. Part of the 31st Virginia had gotten around the left flank of the 3rd (West) Virginia and into it's rear, and it was this detachment that responded to the call.

The 3rd (West) Virginia now occupied some open ground and the woods along the turnpike, and faced the remaining detachment of the 31st Virginia. The Rebels took advantage of the rolling terrain over which the turnpike was built. Shielding themselves behind a small rise in the pike, they would advance until they could just see the Federals in their front, fire from that position and fall back to reload while their comrades would advance to the firing line. After several such volleys, the Federals caught on to what was happening, and held their fire until they saw the heads of the Confederates pop up over the rise, and fired at them.

There was at least one bizarre aspect in this engagement. Company C of the 31st Virginia was recruited from the vicinity of Clarksburg in Western Virginia. Companies B, F and G of the Federal regiment hailed from the identical area. In the prewar years, some members of the opposing companies had been members of the same militia unit. Now, as they faced one another from 100 yards away, old companions were clearly distinguishable as enemies. According to one account: ". . . [the 31st Virginia Infantry] came close to the 3rd, and saluted them, and called them by name, and proceeded with the slaughter."[24]

Use of the word "slaughter" was, in fact, an exaggeration. The 3rd (West) Virginia did not suffer as severely as might have been expected. The relatively few casualties, it was recorded, were due to ". . . the haste with which the enemy fired. The leaden hail went mostly above our heads, and that part (the left) of the regiment referred to as being in the woods, verified this assertion by their appearance when they left the field after the battle, for their caps and shoulders were covered with the bark and buds and twigs of the trees."[25]

Very likely Lieutenant Colonel Thompson of the 3rd (West) Virginia was one of those whose uniform was littered with shreds of bark. The officer had placed a scrap of paper against a tree and was writing a message when a bullet struck the paper, pinning it to the tree. Colonel Thompson, admired for his coolness under fire, was not the least bit disturbed, is said to have remarked dispassionately, "Thank you, I am not posting advertisements, and if I was, I would prefer tacks."[26]

When the remainder of the 31st Virginia left the turnpike and commenced its ascent of Sitlington's Hill, it was replaced on the road by the 21st Virginia. On orders from Jackson, the regiment formed up in a hollow across the road leading to the river. General Jackson further instructed Colonel Richard Cunningham to protect his "men as much as possible and to hold the position at all hazards, and ended by saying in that sharp way of his, 'Tell your men they must hold the road.' "[27]

General Jackson's order was unnecessary. The 21st Virginia was not engaged in the day's fighting, although one man was wounded by a spent ball.[28] Accounts of the fight at McDowell by the 21st Virginia show that there was only some skirmishing along the road after they were ordered into position, therefore it is believed that the 3rd (West) Virginia were pulled back under cover of the woods. The 21st Virginia remained in position here until the close of the fighting, about 8:30 p.m.

When the 31st Virginia disengaged themselves and moved up Sitlington's Hill, they marched at quick-time up a ravine. This was most likely the ravine near where the monument is today located. Before moving out, Sergeant Osborn Wilson later said that he uttered a silent prayer: "God of many help and make us brave and prudent."[29]

Once on top of Sitlington's Hill, they were posted on the right and opened fire on the enemy.

While the 32nd and 82nd Ohio regiments were assailing the right and rear of the 44th Virginia, the 25th and 31st Virginia regiments were ordered into the fight. While the 31st Virginia was engaged on the turnpike when the order came, the exact location of the 25th Virginia cannot be clearly fixed, as it is reported they were being held in reserve. The subsequent moves and posting of the 31st Virginia has already been covered.

High on Sitlington's Hill the action continued without abatement. When the 25th Virginia arrived and took position on the right of the Confederate line, it came immediately under fire. As the fight raged, Colonel George H. Smith, a native of Philadelphia and graduate of V.M.I., spotted movement on Hull's Hill. Northern troops were abandoning the hill and advancing on the turnpike. This meant only one thing to Smith — the Yankees were headed for the path that led to the scene of battle. He relayed the information to Jackson and Johnson. Neither made a response, and Smith's frustration soared to unprecedented heights. Although he had been in service since the spring of 1861, this was his first engagement, and he didn't know how to react.

In his state of annoyance, Smith gazed to his right. There he saw part of the 31st Virginia come over the hill "like a flock of sheep,"[30] march by his flank and quickly go into combat.

During the height of the battle, the Federals spotted a large, shaggy officer waving a hickory walking stick. Recognizing him as the brigade commander, one of the Yankees shouted, "There's old Johnson — let's flank him." The general heard the cry above the crash of shells and the whirr of Minie balls and replied, "Yes, damn you, flank me if you can!"[31]

Another incident that was remembered long after the guns fell silent involved a large Newfoundland dog, the mascot of a Union brigade, that ran back and forth along the line "barking and snapping at the flying missile's." When the casualties were counted at the finish, the dog was among them, pierced by a score of balls.[32]

The name of William G. Kesterson was certain to evoke a chuckle among Confederates when his experience was related in later months. Kesterson was a 19-year-old stone mason from Augusta County who had re-enlisted on May 1 and was in his first battle as a member of the 52nd Virginia. In the fury of the conflict, the private came under the notice of Captain John Humphreys, who was astonished to see the private loading his musket as rapidly as possible and discharging it toward the nearest

65

clouds.

"Billy," cried Humphreys, "there are no Yankees up there."

"No," came the excited answer, "and I'm afraid there never will be."

With that, Billy gained control of himself and took dead aim at the Yankees.[33]

CHAPTER IX
The Battle of McDowell
May 8, 1862 - Phase III

Fighting on Sitlington's Hill accelerated to fever pitch as the sun began its slow descent behind the mountain peaks west of McDowell.

In the center of the Confederate line, the 12th Georgia, with portions of the 44th and 25th Virginia, were battling desperately to repel a series of attacks, their heads silhouetted against the evening sky.

On the left, William C. Scott's brigade was bitterly engaged and had reaped some success. In the same sector, the 52nd Virginia was attempting to flank the Federals. The 31st Virginia was on the extreme right on a wooded hill. The 25th Virginia also was on elevated ground, firing downhill and frequently overshooting their marks.

George Sponaugle of the 25th Virginia was one of those who believed he was on target despite the disadvantages imposed by the hill. He wrote:

> I was a mighty good shot with a gun, as I had used one ever since I had been big enough to carry one. I fired 23 rounds, and some of them were fired at mighty close range. Every time I saw a head I shot at it... I expect I came as near killing some of them as the next one, but it is better that one does not know for certain. It does not weigh so hard on one's mind.[1]

On the opposite side of the firing line, Private Ephraim Hutchison watched his comrades of the 82nd Ohio topple to the ground. His letter revealed:

> They generally [sic] overshot us, their officers could be heard commanding their men to fire low, but our wounded and killed were generally [sic] shot in the head, about the breast and in the arms. Many of the boys had their guns shot to pieces. A ball would strike the stalk and shitter [sic] it, driving the splinters into their hands and faces, they would pick up another gun and go to work as usual.[2]

The 32nd and 82nd Ohio were beginning to exert new pressure on the Confederate right when reinforcements arrived in the form of William B. Taliaferro's Third Brigade. The 10th Virginia, commanded by Simeon B. Gibbons, a Harrisonburg merchant, was the first on the field. It was placed in support of the 52nd Virginia on the left. The 23rd and 37th Virginia were the next regiments to arrive on the crest of the hill.

James H. Wood had been a cadet at the Virginia Military Institute when the war began, and was among those assigned to Richmond as drillmasters in 1861. Two weeks before the clash at McDowell, Wood was commissioned a lieutenant and was serving as adjutant of the 37th Virginia when it was ordered to reinforce Johnson's troops. One of the sights that caught the young officer's eye as he trudged along the Staunton-Parkersburg Turnpike on May 8 was a field hospital. He wrote:

> . . . we found the field hospital, the ground strewn with the wounded, the dead, the dying, and still others came down the ridge from the front, wounded and red with blood, assisted or carried on litters. Surgeons and assistant surgeons are doing all they can to save suffering and life, but the scene is too sickening to pause and consider. On we go up the Ridge, take our position in line and open fire on the enemy. The battle now rages ten times fiercer than before. . .[3]

The 23rd Virginia, on reporting to General Johnson, was assigned to the right of the line in support of the 25th Virginia, which was running low on ammunition, but nevertheless, was stubbornly hanging on. According to the regimental commander, Colonel Alexander G. Taliaferro, the men were "immediately thrown forward and opened a heavy fire upon the enemy in front and on a spur of a hill to the right, and maintained the position handsomely under a terrible fire of musketry and artillery."[4]

Like the 23rd Virginia, the 37th Virginia was positioned on the right upon arriving on the summit of Sitlington's Hill. The unit, commanded by Samuel V. Fulkerson, a prewar circuit court judge in the Old Dominion, was eager to play an important role in the fight and made its presence felt promptly. The 31st Virginia, on the right at the time, was attempting to halt a heavy drive by the Federals trying to take the hill. Fulkerson "interposed it between our troops and the enemy, who were advancing up the slope of the hill; charged and drove them precipitately before him to the base, and then returned with his command to the main field."[5]

Thereafter the 37th Virginia was shifted to the center of the line in support of the 23rd Virginia and the 12th Georgia.

Four companies of the 10th Virginia who had been assisting the 52nd Virginia on the left, were moved to the center to reinforce the 12th Georgia, while the remainder of the regiment shifted to the right to assist the 23rd and 25th Virginia regiments. Later, the 10th Virginia was withdrawn to the vicinity of a sink hole and held in reserve.

When the 12th Georgia, now out of ammunition, pulled back to make room for the 10th Virginia, Captain Thomas J. Gibson of a Georgia company "was deeply impressed with the fine appearance and martial bear-

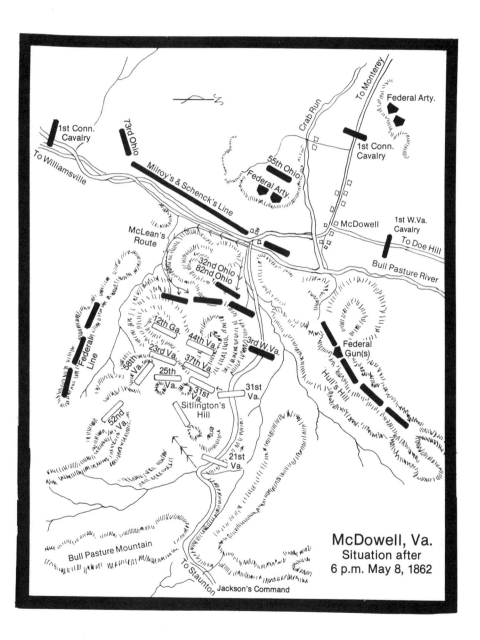

1st Conn. Cavalry

73rd Ohio

To Williamsville

Milroy's & Schenck's Line

Crab Run

To Monterey

Federal Arty.

1st Conn. Cavalry

55th Ohio

Federal Arty.

McLean's Route

McDowell

1st W.Va. Cavalry

To Doe Hill

Bull Pasture River

32nd Ohio

82nd Ohio

Federal Line

12th Ga.

44th Va.

3rd W.Va.

23rd Va.

58th Va.

37th Va.

25th Va.

31st Va.

31st Va.

Sitlington's Hill

Federal Gun(s)

Hull's Hill

52nd Va.

21st Va.

Bull Pasture Mountain

To Staunton

Jackson's Command

McDowell, Va.
Situation after
6 p.m. May 8, 1862

ing of the Tenth Virginia, under the command of Colonel S. B. Gibbons, and with its colors flying. . . Young Gibson said to Colonel Gibbons: 'Give me some ammunition, and I will go back with your regiment,' to which Colonel Gibbons replied, speaking to one of his men, 'Give this young man some ammunition.' " In another article, Captain Gibson stated that the 10th Virginia Infantry advanced "with the precision of a dress parade."[6]

After passing the 12th Georgia, the resolute Virginians proceeded against a withering fire, never halting until they had forced back the Federals and recovered all the ground conceded by the 12th Georgia.

Captain Gibson's praise for the Virginians was unbounded. The incident, he wrote "was one of the handsomest affairs that I witnessed during the war."[7] Before nightfall, 29-year-old Gibbons was dead. He was buried in Harrisonburg.

With the 32nd and 82nd Ohio repelled in their attack on the Confederate right, the two regiments were shifted to the center to help assail the 12th Georgia. From the outset it was apparent that the Georgians were overmatched. Help was an absolute necessity. It arrived in the form of the 23rd Virginia.

Daylight was now receding rapidly. A heavy pall of smoke hung low over the field and fear gripped Edward Johnson, a fear that, under cover of night, the Yankees would attempt to push up the ravine that divided the right and center of his line. The task of preventing such a move was given to the 10th Virginia.

On the left of the Southern line, however, matters were not so orderly. Through the smoke a Yankee flag appeared suddenly in front of the 44th Virginia. Musketry fire was exchanged before the Rebels broke in confusion. Colonel Scott was desperate. The 39-year-old colonel, whose horse had just been shot from under him, rushed forward with hat in hand and shouted to his disorganized troops, asking "if they intended to let the D----d Yankees drive them from their own soil."[8]

The taunt took instant effect. Halting in their tracks, the Virginians whirled and poured a deadly volley into the ranks of the enemy. As the Northerners retreated, Scott's men gave "three cheers for Old Virginia."[9]

Although the outcome of the fighting on Sitlington's Hill was fairly well determined by this hour, Jackson continued to order regiments to the scene of action. John A. Campbell's brigade was marching along the turnpike as Federal artillery shells fell nearby. A short distance from the ravine, a stray bullet struck Major James C. Campbell of the 48th Virginia in the chest. While not mortal, the wound led to the major's early retirement from military service. Seeing Campbell fall, Lieutenant Samuel Hale, the regimental adjutant, rushed to the head of the column and reported the mishap to John Vermillion, the senior captain. The 29-year-old native of Scott County refused command of the regiment, whereupon Hale notified William Hannum, the second ranking captain. The former V.M.I. Cadet also declined the command and suggested that Hale himself take charge of the regiment. Captain Vermillion agreed to this proposal. Reasons for the two captains refusing the command are unknown. Nine days after the battle, on May 17, Vermillion assumed command of the regiment.

About 7:30 o'clock, Jackson ordered the Second Brigade (Campbell's) into the fight. The 42nd Virginia led the way up the precipitous incline and was placed on the wooded hill where the 31st had been the sole defender. By the time the troops took their position darkness mantled the field and the Yankees retired for the night. Despite its inaction, the 42nd Virginia lost three men to artillery fire, one of them wounded mortally.[10]

The 1st Virginia Battalion, the next to arrive on the field, was ordered to join the 42nd Virginia on the right of the line. When the 1st Virginia Battalion arrived on the wooded hill, the men found three companies of the 31st and the 42nd Virginia already in position.[11] The location of the other companies of the 31st and 42nd was not reported.

The 48th Virginia followed the leading units into the main arena. While the regiment was in the process of occupying a hill on the right of the line, Lieutenant Hale sought out Colonel Campbell and explained why he, and not one of the captains, was in command. Colonel Campbell approved of the arrangement and told Hale to obey the orders he had been given.

Moving into position in front of the 58th Virginia, the 48th fired several rounds before Johnson ordered a cease fire. In obedience to orders, the men lay down because they were "under heavy fire. . . the bullets whistling just above us and cutting the bushes. . ."[12]

The deportment of the 48th in its baptism of fire was both good and not-so-good, depending on the source cited. Lieutenant Hale reported: "The. . . regiment seemed entirely self-possessed under fire, and the men fired with a great degree of coolness."[13] Private Andrew J. Johnson, a Scott County farmer who was only two days short of his 24th birthday, thought otherwise. He wrote: "In the first fight we were all scared. . . some of the boys loaded their guns with the bullet end of their cartridges first."[14]

During this exchange, Captain William Greenway of Company F climbed a tree to obtain a better view of the Yankees. He was spotted and subjected to an unexpected volley. The officer made a rapid descent, falling to the ground. He was unhurt.[15] Captain Greenway resigned a short time later because of "the diminished number of my company." The brigade commander "approved & heartily recommended" the action due to "the officer's incompetence."[16]

Private Martin W. Brett of the 12th Georgia was not as fortunate as Greenway. He described his reaction after being wounded in the left arm:

Soon after being shot I was seized with the most intense craving for water I had ever felt. It seemed as though my insides were burning out. I stood several minutes watching other men fall near me. I heard others calling for water. I did so too, but there was no one to supply our wants. I watched the blood spout freely from my arm. Very soon the gray mountain rocks turned green. The mountains seemed to spin around in the air like a boy's toy top. My desire for water overcame all pain caused by the wound, and I staggered back about fifty paces to a little branch we had fought over about an hour before. The water was cool and refreshing and I drank my fill.[17]

A doctor found Brett and dressed his wound with raw cotton, and left him. Brett was sent to a hospital in Staunton the next day to recover.

General Edward Johnson was another late-hour casualty on May 8. About 8 o'clock, "Old Alleghany" was wounded in the ankle and turned command of the field over to General Taliaferro. The wounded general was assisted from the field and, on arriving at the turnpike found Jackson in conversation with Jed Hotchkiss. General Johnson reported to Jackson the conditions on Sitlington's Hill and then moved on to a field hospital.[18]

Hotchkiss, who had located a road suitable for moving artillery around McDowell, as requested by Jackson, had returned to Wilson's Hotel about dark and was taking his ease when he heard for the first time the sound of combat on Sitlington's Hill.[19] Why the engineer had not heard the sound of firing earlier is difficult to understand, because it was clearly audible to troops at Franklin, Crab Bottom (Blue Grass) and those east of the Bull Pasture Mountain.

Regardless of the reasons, Hotchkiss called for his horse and encountered Jackson near the ravine leading to the crest of Sitlington's Hill. In the enveloping darkness, Jackson asked his aide to climb the hill and instruct Taliaferro to hold his position until the Stonewall Brigade arrived.[20]

Hotchkiss turned the reins of his horse over to a soldier standing nearby with orders to hold him until he returned.

On the summit, Hotchkiss found a general state of confusion. Officers were shouting orders, troops were trying to obey orders, others were attempting to care for the wounded. Having delivered his message to Taliaferro, Hotchkiss descended the hill and rejoined Jackson. The two rode back to Wilson's Hotel. In parting company for the night, Jackson reminded Hotchkiss to have the artillery in position by 3 a.m., a sure indication that "Old Jack" expected the battle to be resumed May 9.[21]

The First Brigade (Stonewall Brigade), commanded by General Charles S. Winder, though ordered into the fight on Sitlington's Hill, never made it that far. By the time they drew close to the battlefield, darkness had settled over the land, and they could clearly see the periodic bursts of flame from the Federal artillery posted on Hull's Hill.

Along the Federal lines, by 8:30 p.m., the officers and men were ready to call it a day. The troops, who had received 60 rounds of ammunition each before entering the fray, were now out of cartridges, or nearly so, and Milroy issued the recall order "having achieved the purpose of the attack."[22]

Before the recall was issued, General Schenck learning of the shortage of ammunition on Sitlington's Hill, made arrangements to re-supply them. Three wagon loads of ammunition were started forward on the turnpike, but ran into a problem. The only way to get the ammunition to the men, was by putting it into haversacks and carrying it up the hill. The wagons returned to camp.

Along about this same time, the 5th (West) Virginia was ordered to march up the turnpike, to the aid of the other troops, if necessary, but no aid was needed by then.[23]

As darkness settled over the combatants, their firing provided quite a spectacular show for the Federal troops at McDowell. Frank S. Reader, a post war newspaper editor, wrote:

> The flashing of the guns after nightfall on the mountain side and crest, amid the trees, was indescribably grand and beautiful, and no one witnessing it can ever forget it. At times sheets of flame shot from the angry mouths of the guns, lighting up the whole mountain side, and again the flash from one or a few muskets made a scene of particular beauty and animation.[24]

Having received the recall order, Colonel McLean formed the 75th Ohio where they would be out of the heaviest of the Rebel fire, then marched to the base of Sitlington's Hill. There, he halted and faced his men toward the Confederates should they decide to follow. Now, the three other Ohio regiments made their way down the hill, the 32nd Ohio bringing up the rear. All four regiments had brought most of their dead and wounded off the field as they withdrew. Once they had all reached the base of Sitlington's Hill, they were joined by the 3rd (West) Virginia. Thus, all in one body, they marched back to their camps on the opposite side of the Bull Pasture River. On the heights above them, the battle-weary Federals could hear the ringing cry of the Rebels for "Davis and the Confederacy," echoing over the blood stained field.

General Milroy, writing to his wife, explained that his men, though out of ammunition, were determined to hold their positions until a fresh supply could be brought up. Because of their fatigued condition, however, Milroy considered it prudent that they be withdrawn. The general placed his loss as 240 killed and wounded and estimated that the Confederate loss was greater as his troops were armed with Enfield rifles and "were good marksmen."[25]

The Battle of McDowell was over, having lasted four hours. Back at McDowell, Union troops occupied their old camp sites, ate supper and went to sleep on the ground. Two companies of the 2nd (West) Virginia (Companies B and D) were posted as pickets on the turnpike, where they remained until the retreat began.

One Yankee entertained a ray of hope for the morrow, writing in his diary, "Rumor is that Gen. Banks is coming up in their rear."[26] The rumor was without validity, of course, because Banks at that very moment was in the Shenandoah Valley, fortifying Strasburg.

The only official report of casualties in the 82nd Ohio was an unpublished account revealing that about 120 members had their uniforms pierced by bullets. In addition, several had their clothing slashed by bayonets.[27] When the blouse and pants of the colonel were pierced by bullets, ". . . he would curse the rebels to take better aim than that. . ."[28] A member of the 82nd Ohio, writing about the battle, stated that the casualties in that regiment were five killed, perhaps six. The sixth man, the writer stated, could have been taken prisoner. The account went on to state that about 20 of the 82nd Ohio were wounded, and by May 21, at least three of those had died as a result of their wounds.[29] A post war thesis on the Battle of McDowell mentioned that the casualties in the 82nd Ohio were higher than those of the other regiments engaged, since it had been caught in a cross fire.[30]

The heaviest loss on the Confederate side was sustained by the 12th Georgia. Joseph Snider, a member of the 31st Virginia, wrote in his diary that the 12th Georgia had fought like tigers, but had suffered dreadfully.[31] The loss in the 25th Virginia was likewise heavy, being second only to that of the Georgians.

In the immediate aftermath of the battle, Colonel Michael G. Harman, who had been wounded in the arm, inspected the battlefield. The former quartermaster of Jackson's army described his experiences: "It was a desperate fight, and I wish you could see the battle ground. The trees, bushes and twigs are cut all to pieces. . . the wonder is how any body got off alive."[32]

Joseph Snider of the 31st Virginia visited the scene of carnage on May 14 when the army was on its return march from Franklin. He noted:

"Stopped about an hour on the battlefield. There were almost two acres that was almost mowed by the bullets. There was bushes six inches in diameter that was cut by bullets until they fell down."[33]

Brigadier General Edward "Alleghany" Johnson, C. S. Army.

Major-General Thomas J. "Stonewall" Jackson, C.S. Army.

Brigadier General Robert Houston Milroy, U. S. Army.

Major-General John C. Fremont, U. S. Army.

Brigadier General Robert S. Schenck, U. S. Army.

Monument along Rt. 250, May 1989, which reads: Commemorating The Battle of McDowell, May 8, 1862. Federals in action - 4,000. Killed and Wounded - 256. Confederates in action - 2,500. Killed and Wounded - 498. Confederate Officer Killed - Captains: Samuel Dawson; William L. Furlow; John McMillan and James W. Patterson. Lieutenant's: John K. Goldwire; William A. Massie; William H. Turpin and Joseph T. Woodward, all of the 12th Georgia Regiment. Colonel S. P. Gibbons, 10th Virginia Regiment; Captain J. Whitmore, 25th Virginia Regiment; Lieut. William H. Gregory, 52nd Virginia Regiment; Lieut. Charles E. Dyer, 25th Virginia Regiment; Lieut. Samuel P. Dye, 37th Virginia Regiment; Lieut. C. G. Fletcher, 37th Virginia Regiment and Lieut. John A. Carson, 52nd Virginia Regiment. Erected By The Highland Chapter United Daughters of the Confederacy, 1917.

Marker along Rt. 250, May 1989.

View of the Ravine used by General Johnson's men. This is toward the half-way point, May 1989.

Top of Sitlington's Hill, looking toward McDowell, May 1989.

View of Sitlington's Hill as seen from the Union Artillery Position. The open area near the upper center of the photograph is part of the battle line, May 1989.

View of the Ravine leading to the top of Sitlington's Hill, May 1989.

View of the battlefield, Confederate Right Flank, May 1989.

Monument located in front of the Presbyterian Church in McDowell, May 1989.

IN THIS AREA ARE BURIED
CONFEDERATE AND UNION
SOLDIERS WHO DIED AT
MCDOWELL VA - MAY 8 1862

Marker located in the church cemetery in McDowell, across the road from the church, May 1989.

Looking from Sitlington's Hill toward McDowell, May 1989.

View of the Ravine leading to the battlefield, near the monument on Rt. 250, May 1989.

View of the McDowell Battlefield from an old postcard. Author's Collection.

Another view of the McDowell Battlefield as shown on an old postcard.

CHAPTER X

May 9 to 14, 1862

As morning winds pushed back the smoke. . .
brave men stood and cried. . .
the battle was over and they had won . . .
but many a friend had died.

"The Battle of McDowell," D. Durant.

As the night-time hours dragged by, William B. Taliaferro reposition-ed regiments so that the field could be held against fresh attacks in the morning. Troops were placed beyond Federal view in ravines and gullies. Skirmishers and pickets were thrown forward while other weary fighters refilled their cartridge boxes. Near midnight many regiments returned to their wagons in the Cow Pasture River Valley to rest and refresh them-selves.

Simultaneously, the Stonewall Brigade and the V.M.I. Cadets, the rear elements of Jackson's column, put in an appearance and were assign-ed the grisley task of bringing the dead and wounded off the battlefield.[1]

In daylight it would have been a repugnant chore. In the dead of night it was sheer terror as litter bearers stumbled and fell over rocks in the steep declivities, and shouts and groans of the wounded rent the air.

The dead were laid in the rear of the line. Charles C. Wight of the 58th Virginia stopped by to pay final respects to old comrades and made this memorandum: "It was indeed a sight to be remembered, that long line of pale faces turned up to the bright moon which rendered their paleness more ghostly and the expression more startling."[2]

Hampered by the rugged terrain, and with only the moon to il-luminate it, Confederate details began the doleful task of ministering to the wounded and locating the dead. In addition, orders were issued to col-lect the fallen weapons from the field, both their own and those left behind by the Federals. Detailed for that purpose were the 25th, 42nd and 48th Virginia, along with the V.M.I. Cadets and the Stonewall Brigade. Through the cold, dreary night they labored until, near dawn, they were permitted to take a recess for food and rest.

In McDowell, Robert H. Milroy ordered out strong pickets and skir-mishers. He also interrogated Rebel captives and deserters, about 50 of whom had turned themselves in. They told the general that Stonewall Jackson had 20 pieces of artillery and was expecting reinforcements momentarily. The information was speciaous, but Milroy accepted it at face value. He convened a council of war, at which time it was decided unanimously to retreat to Franklin.³

At 11:30 p.m. Robert C. Schenck sent a dispatch to Colonel Albert Tracy, informing John Fremont's assistant adjutant general that wagons loaded with stores and wounded soldiers were withdrawing from McDowell. The troops, he added, would move at 2 o'clock.⁴

The men were awakened at 1 a.m. and were told they had one hour to prepare to move. In the meantime, however, much work remained to be done. Because all the wagons had departed, commissary stores on the western edge of town had to be destroyed. Ammunition that was not dumped into Crab Run was burned. Tents and "hard bread" were put to the torch. Other material such as camp equipage and cases of Enfield rifles, as well as sutlers stores and 180 head of cattle stolen from Robert A. Glendy were left behind. Also left behind was the Federal dead, and a number of soldiers that were taken prisoner when the Confederates occupied McDowell on May 9.

The exodus from McDowell began at 2 a.m. sharp and was done so quietly, said a member of the 73rd Ohio, "that the enemy did not know of it until the morning revealed our burning and deserted camps."⁵ The 25th Ohio and a squadron of the 1st Battalion Connecticut Cavalry brought up the rear of the column.

The Federals marched along the Crab Run road until 8 a.m. on the morning of May 9, at which time they halted near the Forks of the Waters. By now they were some 12 miles from McDowell, and they set up a temporary field hospital on the Vandevender farm. General Schenck took a defensive posture while at this location, expecting the Rebels to attack.

At 3 a.m., one hour after the Yankees began their withdrawal, Jed Hotchkiss left Jackson's headquarters at Wilson's Hotel and rode to the top of Bull Pasture Mountain. A short distance farther, he learned from Rebel pickets that the enemy had evacuated McDowell.

As Hotchkiss chatted with the pickets they were joined by another horseman. He was colonel Robert Sitlington, on whose property the battle had been fought. The colonel confirmed that the Federals were gone and told the topographical engineer, "I thank God that you have so punished the insolent foe that has been tyranizing over us."⁶

After sending word to Jackson of the Yankee retreat, Hotchkiss rode to the battlefield where he made sketches to use later in preparing his maps of the battle. While thus engaged, Hotchkiss discovered a number of Yankee dead scattered over the battlefield.

The Confederate dead had been removed from the field during the night and carried down the ravine. At the bottom of Sitlington's Hill, the dead were laid out on the grass along side the road. In the 1920's, the remains of a Confederate were discovered among the rocks of Sitlington's Hill and buried with full military honors.

Having completed his notes on the battlefield, Hotchkiss rejoined Jackson, who had moved his headquarters to the home of Mrs. Felix Hull in McDowell. Before arriving there, however, Jackson had ordered cavalry into the village to clean out any possible Union malingerers. The expedition yielded several privates, a group of negroes and the lieutenant colonel of the 75th Ohio. Colonel Constable, it seems, had gone to a house west of McDowell to get some rest. A cousin of the colonel was supposed to inform him when the retreat commenced. Somehow the kinsman forgot it.[7]

That same morning, May 9, Colonel John D. Imboden informed Jackson that he planned to ride to Staunton, where he had been a lawyer prior to 1861. Could he be of service to the general while he was there? Yes, he could. General Jackson would be most appreciative if Imboden would send a message to Richmond for him. The general made several attempts at drafting a telegram. After ripping up each piece of paper, he wrote a message he deemed satisfactory. He handed it to Imboden with the request that it be sent from Staunton. Later, the colonel unfolded the paper and read:

Valley District, Va., May 9, 1862.
Via Staunton, Va., May 10, 1862.

General S. Cooper,
    Adjutant-General:
    God blessed our arms with victory at McDowell yesterday.

T. J. Jackson,
Major-General.[8]

While Imboden is generally accorded the distinction of carrying Jackson's telegram to Staunton, there is one dissenting voice. It belongs to Oren F. Morton. In his book, the *History of Highland County,* Morton contends that the actual bearer of the good tidings was Andrew W. Gillett of the 52nd Virginia.[9]

As members of the Valley Army filtered into McDowell in the early hours of May 9, they concentrated first of all on the Yankee plunder. The "hard bread" left undamaged was like ambrosia to the famished Rebels, who devoured it post haste. Ten members of the 73rd Ohio also fell into Confederate hands. Their colonel had been unable to locate them when the evacuation began in the early hours of darkness. Besides these, a number of seriously wounded Federals, unable to be moved, fell into the hands of the Rebels. Twelve Federal dead were discovered in the Presbyterian Church, others in the Bradshaw Hotel and private homes. According to one soldier, "every one of them [had been] shot in the head."[10]

It was also alleged that a number of Union dead had been burned when the commissary stores were put to the torch. Sergeant William Montgomery of the 33rd Virginia insisted that the Yankees had piled about 50 corpses near the battlefield, covered them with brush and leaves and ignited them. Montgomery revealed that some of them were still alive when the pyre was set afire.[11]

B. A. Colonna, one of the V.M.I. Cadets who assisted in the burial of the Union dead, described his experience: "On going to the brick house [Hull's] we found that the parlor had been used as a hospital; there was a dead man laid on top of the piano, and in the dining-room on the table there was a litter with a man on it." The soldier was still breathing, with his brain exposed, but died a short time later."[12]

The Federal dead were buried on a low bluff on the side of the turnpike, the Confederates near the ravine they had ascended the previous day. Some Confederates were sent home for interment. This was particularly true of members of the 12th Georgia and some Virginia regiments.

While the bodies of the dead were being prepared for burial, some Confederates, hard-pressed for footwear, were apprehended removing the shoes of Federals. In one instance, the colonel commanding the Cadets caught a man snipping the buttons from the coat of a dead Yankee.[13]

In 1866, the Federal dead were removed to the National Cemetery in Staunton, and the Confederate dead to the Thornrose Cemetery in the same city.

As soon as Jackson determined that the Federals were in retreat he ordered the cavalry companies of Captains George Sheetz and John Q. Winfield to give chase. The Cadets not assigned to the burial detail were placed in charge of the prisoners and captured property. Late on May 9, Jackson reviewed his victorious troops.

Lieutenant Colonel Alexander C. Jones also received orders from Jackson. The V.M.I. graduate and prewar judge in St. Paul was directed to take his cavalry to Cheat Mountain, 100 miles from Staunton.[14]

When the retreating Federal column halted the day after the battle, it was about five miles from Monterey. From there 20 members of the 55th Ohio commanded by Lieutenant R. F. Patrick, fanned out as pickets on the Seybert farm. While in that position, they were attacked by Sheetz and Winfield. The noon-time skirmish was brief and the Yankees fell back, leaving six men, one of them wounded, in the hands of the Confederates.[15]

When Schenck learned of the engagement, he took immediate steps to receive an expected full-scale attack. Artillery was placed on the Rymer Hills at the junction of the Strait Creek and Monterey roads. Infantry was sent out on each road. Other troops took position on the Beverage Hill, east of the Thorny Bottom Church, to guard the Doe Hill road.[16]

While awaiting a Rebel assault, Schenck wired Fremont, explaining that he had halted to give his weary men an opportunity to rest and added, "If you have support near enough advance them to me at once."[17]

Several hours passed without an attack. About 2 o'clock the march resumed along the Strait Creek road, under handicaps. Southern sympathizers along the route had felled trees across the road and placed other obstacles in the path of the bluecoats. The obstructions forced the Yankees to abandon wagons and some artillery along the way.[18] The Federals camped that evening about nine miles from Franklin, having covered 23 miles during the day.

Even with the Federals in retreat, estimates of Jackson's military capabilities varied widely in his ranks. Osborn Wilson thought that "his men have the greatest confidence in his efficiency and ability."[19] Major John A. Harman, the hard-driving, hard-swearing quartermaster chief, wrote on the day after the battle: "We have been worsted by mismanagement. I am more than ever satisfied of Jackson's incompetency. . . .We have the battle-field but no victory. Our loss has been severe and heavy."[20]

The Confederate pursuit on May 10, of the vanquised foe continued without abatement along the dusty road leading westward. When Jackson and his staff arrived at the Seybert farm, the general felt the need for a drink of water. Dismounting, he walked toward the house, where he spotted a lad on the porch completely engrossed in the passing spectacle. The sight prompted "Old Jack" to offer some fatherly advice. Recalling his own dawn-to-dark work schedule as a boy in Western Virginia, the general informed the youth that his time could be spent to greater advantage working in the fields than by watching bedraggled graycoats on the march.[21]

Between 3 and 4 o'clock, while the army was enjoying one of its hourly rests, Jackson summoned Jed Hotchkiss to his side. Together, they rode into the woods where Hotchkiss was instructed to take some cavalry and barricade the roads through North River and Dry River gaps to prevent Nathaniel P. Banks from leaving the Shenandoah Valley to reinforce Milroy, or vice versa. Hotchkiss was to have those gaps blocked by daylight of May 11, and was ordered to take a string of couriers with him, so he could report his progress to Jackson every hour.

Late that night, Hotchkiss arrived at Churchville west of Staunton, where he met with Captain Frank F. Sterrett of the Churchville Cavalry. The junior officer was directed to have his men mounted and ready to ride at 3 o'clock on the morning of May 11.[22] Captain Sterrett and his men were ready at the appointed hour. Before daylight the mission was accomplished.

While Hotchkiss was thus engaged, two companies of the 7th Virginia Cavalry under Captains John C. Shoup and Thomas B. Massie were blockading the road at Brock's Gap and the road from Shaw's Fork to Franklin in an identical manner.

Near sundown on May 10, Jackson's command went into camp at the Forks of the Waters.

General Schenck, at the same time, was continuing his steady tramp toward Franklin, bivouacking the night of May 11 about two miles south of the town. Once "Camp Milroy" was occupied, Schenck sent detachments from his command out to meet the advancing Rebels. In early afternoon Schenck discovered that his telegraph line had been broken. As related in Chapter VI, this was the work of Captain E. W. Boggs of the 25th Virginia, but Schenck was convinced that citizens were the real culprits. As a result of this, Reverend Ambrose Meadows was shot down and killed by Federal troops.

When Jackson resumed his chase of the Yankees on the morning of May 11, he found visibility obscured by billowing black smoke. This was the handiwork of Schenck, who ordered his men to set afire hay ricks, rail fences and woodland bordering each side of the road. The smoke slowed the Rebel's pace perceptibly, but Jackson undoubtedly appreciated the stratagem and made a mental note of it for possible future use.

General Jackson encountered no strong resistance until he reached Trout Rock, a few miles from Franklin where he was fired upon by sharpshooters ensconced in rocks above the narrow passage. Customarily, when hard work was at hand, the general called upon the Stonewall Brigade, which he had led to immortality at First Manassas. Fortunately, the brigade was at the front of his column, so "Old Jack" asked Charles S. Winder, the brigade commander, to select a regiment to dislodge the sharpshooters. General Winder chose the 4th Virginia, which proceeded into the defile, only to return moments later.

Next, a member of Jackson's staff ascended a nearby hill and reported the Yankees in full retreat. Captain John Q. Winfield's Company of the 7th Virginia Cavalry was directed to clear the way. It made a gallant attempt, but came back with one wounded horseman and minus two mounts. Another company from the same cavalry regiment, Captain John L. Knott's, was asked to undertake the same assignment. Like the others, it too was driven back.

By this time, Jackson's patience was running low. Could none of his command clear the passage of Union sharpshooters? The redoubtable Harry Gilmor, then attached to the 7th Virginia Cavalry, agreed to the challenge. The captain chose ten men, instructing them to watch closely for a signal from him as they proceeded. The group advanced, deployed as skirmishers, and drew enemy fire as had the others. Then Gilmor detected a slackening of fire. That was the moment for the signal. The men charged, clearing the pass and capturing four Yankees.[23]

With the road free of bluecoats, Jackson waved his column forward. It advanced rapidly until, within two miles of Franklin, Schenck's entire command was encountered in battle formation across the narrow valley. One of Schenck's Parrot guns fired five shells at the Confederates without noticeable damage. The major losers were members of a family who were escaping through a vegetable garden when a shell struck their log home behind them, reducing it to splinters.

General Jackson replied to Schenck's fire. The old artillerist ordered up his guns, which achieved quick results. The Federals retreated and the Valley Army went into camp at McCoy's Mill, a couple of miles from Franklin. General Jackson made his headquarters at the home of Henry Simmons, ten miles south of Franklin. Throughout the evening of May 11, the two armies skirmished with each other.

At his headquarters in Franklin, Schenck busied himself writing dispatches to Fremont, now in Petersburg. One of his messages informed the Mountain Department commander: "Finding the arrival of re-enforcements so uncertain, I am moving my whole force to-day to the hill at the town of Franklin, 2 miles."[24]

In another missive, Schenck advised his superior, "I expect to be attacked in force, and on perhaps more than one side."[25]

In his reply, Adjutant Tracy said: "If you can fall back in safety, do so until you reach us. If not, hold the place, improving its natural defenses... Every exertion will be made to arrive in time with our entire force."[26]

Nearly two hours later, about 7:30 p.m., Schenck informed Fremont that he thought it better to remain at Franklin then to retreat farther. General Schenck also asked Fremont to come up as quickly as possible and wondered how soon he might arrive. Within an hour, Schenck had his answer. Because of the exhausted condition of Louis Blenker's wandering warriors, he was told, the advance from Petersburg could not begin before 3 a.m. on May 12. As it turned out, Fremont did not reach Franklin until the morning of May 13, and his troops one day later.

When Fremont's troops entered the village, they found the brigades of Schenck and Milroy on Friend's Hill on the northern outskirts of the town.[27]

While the Federals were looking apprehensively over their shoulders, expecting an attack at almost any moment, Jackson, as was his custom after a battle, called for a day of prayer and thanksgiving for the victory at McDowell in gratitude "to Almighty God for thus having crowned your arms with success, and in praying that he will continue to lead you from victory to victory until a independence shall be established, and make us that people whose God is the Lord."[28]

The divine services, which began about 10 o'clock on Monday, May 12, were barely over when a courier dashed up to Jackson in mid-afternoon and handed him a message. The general read it, scribbled a note and handed it to a chaplain, who read it, "and then, raising his hands said abruptly: 'Receive the benediction.' "[29]

The communique was from General Joseph E. Johnston. The commander of the Army of Northern Virginia, which was defending Richmond against George B. McClellan's Army of the Potomac, ordered Jackson back into the Shenandoah Valley. There he was to join forces with General Ewell and attack Banks. Such a maneuver would prevent Banks from crossing the Blue Ridge and occupying Fredericksburg, thereby freeing Irvin McDowell to march from that place and reinforce McClellan with his 40,000-man I Corps.

If Jackson were unable to fulfill this order, Johnston added, he should plan to join Johnston or J. R. Anderson at Fredericksburg.[30]

The retreat from Franklin began immediately. Before turning his column southward, however, Jackson issued an order to Harry Gilmor, instructing him to remain behind with two cavalry companies, keep the camp fires burning and make frequent dashes into Franklin to deceive the enemy regarding the Confederate withdrawal. The Rebels encamped the night of May 12 on the farm of Henry Simmons.

The next morning Jackson dashed off a memo to General Ewell, apprising "Old Bald Head" at Swift Run Gap that he was on his way back. That night, Jackson's regiments bivouacked at Wimer's Mill on Strait Creek, six miles from Monterey.

Captain Harry Gilmor, on May 15 was relieved of his rear guard duties and was replaced by a company of the 7th Virginia Cavalry under Captain Thomas S. Davis. Subsequently, Gilmor was ordered to scout west of Shenandoah Mountain and to harass Fremont whenever possible.

As General Fremont left Franklin on May 15, for the Shenandoah Valley to assist Banks, Captain Gilmor struck one final blow. The captain with 26 of his men charged Fremont's rear guard and took 18 of them prisoner, along with their weapons and other property, sustaining the loss of one trooper wounded. In the town of Franklin, Gilmor paroled 256 sick and wounded Yankees. Finished with that, Gilmor pursued Fremont's army until the latter turned onto the Wardensville road.[31]

Few marches during the entire war were conducted under such intolerable conditions as prevailed on Jackson's return to the Valley. Torrential rains that commenced on May 12 continued intermittently for the next five days. Shoes turned to shreds and men trudged through the mud barefooted because there was no other footwear available. Clothing, blankets and firewood were drenched and what few provisions the men had were damaged by the water. Wagons broke down, spilling their contents into the mire, and pure drinking water was not to be found.

Under those adverse conditions, the mood of the men turned sour. Voices rose in protest. Strident epithets permeated the ranks, and rebellion festered in the 27th Virginia.

When the army was near McDowell, the 12-month enlistment of many members of that regiment expired and they threw down their arms, announcing their plans to return home. Colonel Andrew Jackson Grigsby appealed to Jackson for instructions.

The general viewed the incident for what it was. In a rage, he stormed, "What is this but mutiny? "Why does Colonel Grigsby refer to me to know what to do with mutiny. He should shoot them where they stand."[32]

Major Robert L. Dabney, Jackson's chief of staff, penned a quick reply to Grigsby. The colonel was ordered to parade the mutineers before their regimental comrades, explain the nature of their offense, and offer them an opportunity to return to duty. Those that refused to do so were to be shot on the spot. Given that alternative, the dissidents picked up their rifles and grudgingly returned to duty. Nothing more was heard from them.[33]

A heavy downpour greeted Jackson's weary troops on the morning of May 14 as they sloshed toward McDowell. For Jackson, the gloom was lifted by a message from Robert E. Lee in which the military advisor to President Davis congratulated him for the "handsome and energetic manner in which you have driven the enemy and achieved a victory."[34]

General Jackson spent that night in the home of Mrs. Felix Hull, as he had done earlier, while his men camped at Shaw's Fork east of McDowell. From there, one soldier wrote: "Our heads are turned now towards Staunton, but where we are bound I can not say."[35]

CHAPTER XI

May 15 to May 18, 1862

Early on the morning of May 15, Stonewall Jackson issued an order for Jedediah Hotchkiss to ride to the head of the column and direct William Taliaferro to march his brigade toward Jenning's Gap and Stribling Springs rather than toward Staunton.

Hotchkiss delivered the message, then proceeded to Lebanon Springs where he secured lodging for Jackson and his staff at a place identified only as King's.[1]

Before leaving McDowell, Jackson also composed two messages. One was to General Ewell, advising the division commander at Swift Run Gap that his brigades would be within 30 miles of Harrisonburg that evening. The second communication was addressed to authorities in Richmond recommending that Edward Johnson be promoted to the rank of major general ". . . for his gallant and meritorious conduct in the battle near McDowell. . ."[2]

General Johnson's promotion was slow to materialize. He was required to participate in many more battles before the higher rank was approved on February 28, 1863.

Later in the day Jackson ordered prisoners, deserters and disloyal citizens taken under guard to Staunton.[3]

Also, on May 15, Jackson's command was diminished by 200 men. The V.M.I. Cadets, who had joined the army at Staunton nearly two weeks before, were ordered back to Lexington by the Board of Visitors. It was a sad moment of parting for the general and the Cadets. Though the young soldiers had seen no action, they had expected to follow their old professor to future glories. They departed the Valley Army at Lebanon White Sulphur Springs with Jackson's praises ringing in their ears.[4]

General Jackson's army remained in camp on Friday, May 16, in compliance with Jefferson Davis's proclamation setting aside that day for prayer and fasting throughout the Confederacy. Some troops agreed that there was a need for prayer, but fasting? They had been doing that for days.

For many men, every step on the eastward march intensified their grief. They had joined the army to defend their homes and families in the mountains of Western Virginia. Now they were marching in the opposite direction, into the Shenandoah Valley. This movement violated a basic trust with their government, they felt, and exposed kinfolk to the depredations of northern invaders. William H. Hull of the 31st Virginia was a member of that group. The dark-complexioned resident of Pocahontas County wrote: "The men . . . were greatly disappointed when we were called on to turn our backs on our homes and the dear ones we had left behind us."[5]

The army marched again on Saturday, May 17. The head of the column arrived at North River, opposite Bridgewater, that evening. The rear encamped near Mount Solon.

Very early on Sunday, May 18, Jackson greeted an unexpected visitor. He was Richard S. Ewell, who had ridden from Swift Run Gap laden with woes and perplexities. When Jackson left him on April 30, Ewell was ordered to keep an eye on Banks at Harrisonburg. If the Union general advanced toward Staunton, Ewell was to strike him in flank and rear. While Jackson was out of touch, Banks had moved, but it was down the Valley and in the opposite direction from Staunton.

Furthermore, Ewell had been bombarded by all sorts of suggestions from Joseph E. Johnston and Robert E. Lee in Richmond. He was told to thus and if this or that took place. General Jackson, his immediate superior, was somewhere in the western wilds, he knew not where. "Old Bald Head" was befuddled, and more than a little angry, when he rode up to Jackson's tent and approached the officer whom, a few days earlier, he had referred to as "crazy" and "an idiot."

Ewell laid his frustrations before Jackson, who listened politely. When Ewell finished, "Old Jack" said he thought he knew how to proceed.

Two days earlier he had received a letter from Robert E. Lee in which the writer said: "Whatever movement you make against Banks do it speedily, and if successful drive him back toward the Potomac, and create the impression, as far as practicable that you design threatening that line."[6]

There was the solution to Ewell's predicament. The two armies would unite, drive the Northern hordes from the Valley and, as Lee suggested, create the impression of threatening the Potomac.

The union of the two forces was still several days away, but Ewell was in a far gentler spirit when he rode back to his camp that night than he had been at daybreak.

Afer the two generals had concluded their conference and mapped plans for their operation against Banks, Ewell accepted an invitation to accompany Jackson and his staff to divine service. Attendance at a religious meeting was alien to Ewell, who had not yet become the practicing Christian he was a year later. But, on this bright spring morning, "Old Bald Head" sat in rapt attention as Robert L. Dabney preached on the text:

"Come unto me, all ye that labor and are heavy laden, and I will give you rest."

The text seemed particularly appropriate for those who had just completed the rigorous McDowell Campaign, and were about to embark on marches and battles every bit as severe.

APPENDICES

Tables of Casualties
Battle of McDowell

The following tables were compiled from various wartime and post war sources. It is likely that the totals were slightly higher, as there are no reports for those units engaged in skirmishing during the early part of the battle.

Federal Casualties

Regiment	Killed*	Wounded	Captured	Total
32nd Ohio Inf.	7	49	1	57
3rd (W.) Va. Inf.	5	41	1	47
25th Ohio Inf.	6	51	1	58
75th Ohio Inf.	6	32	1	39
82nd Ohio Inf.	9	47	1	57
Hyman's Battery	1	——	——	1
2nd (W.) Va. Inf.	No Report for skirmishers		——	——
73rd Ohio Inf.	No Report for skirmishers		——	——
Total	34	220	5**	259

*The figures for killed include those mortally wounded.

**Official Records show only three missing. These three were supposed to belong to the 75th Ohio, and were thought to be among those killed.

Confederate Casualties

Regiment	Killed*	Wounded	Captured	Total
Valley Army First Brigade	Not engaged			
Second Brigade				
21st Virginia Inf.	1	1	——	2
42nd Virginia Inf.	1	2	——	3
48th Virginia Inf.	1	3	——	4
1st Va. Battn. Inf.	1	1	——	2
Total	4	7	——	11
Third Brigade				
10th Virginia Inf.	4	17	——	21
23rd Virginia Inf.	10	31	——	41
37th Virginia Inf.	12	27	——	39
Total	26	75	——	101

Army of the Northwest

Field and Staff	——	1	——	1
12th Georgia Inf.**	52	123	——	175
25th Virginia Inf.	23	53	——	76
31st Virginia Inf.	6	16	——	22
44th Virginia Inf.	5	14	——	19
52nd Virginia Inf.	14	59	——	73
58th Virginia Inf.	16	34	——	50
Unknown Regiments	——	——	4***	4
Total	116	300	4	416
Grand Total	146	382	4	532

*Figures for killed include those mortally wounded.

**Post war accounts show 240 killed and wounded in the 12th Georgia, more than one third the number engaged.

***General Milroy reported that five men had been taken prisoner, and that a number of deserters had surrendered.

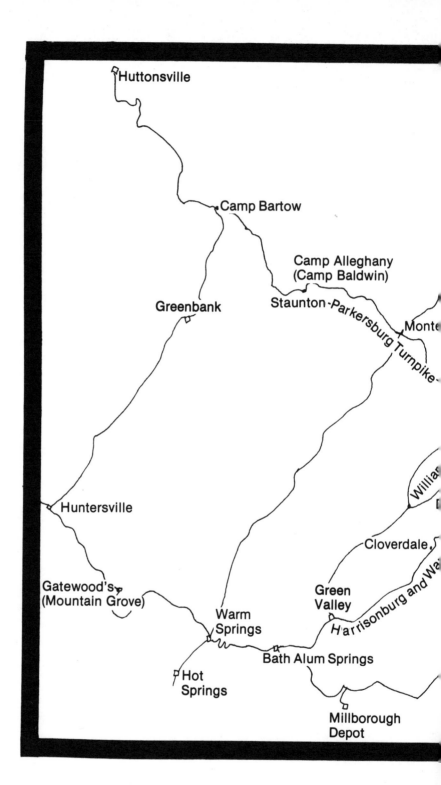

Huttonsville

Camp Bartow

Camp Alleghany
(Camp Baldwin)

Staunton-Parkersburg Turnpike

Monte

Greenbank

Willia

Huntersville

Cloverdale

Gatewood's
(Mountain Grove)

Green
Valley

Harrisonburg and Wa

Warm
Springs

Bath Alum Springs

Hot
Springs

Millborough
Depot

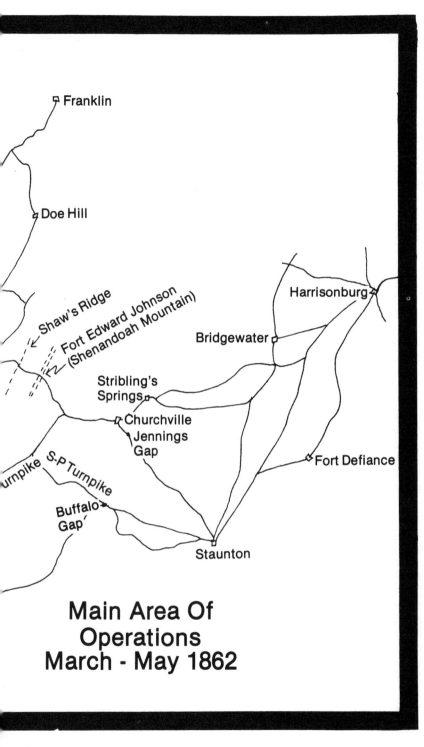

Franklin

Doe Hill

Shaw's Ridge

Fort Edward Johnson
(Shenandoah Mountain)

Harrisonburg

Bridgewater

Stribling's Springs

Churchville

Jennings Gap

Fort Defiance

Turnpike

S-P Turnpike

Buffalo Gap

Staunton

Main Area Of Operations
March - May 1862

ENDNOTES

Chapter I

1. Allan Nevis, *Fremont: The West's Greatest Adventurer* (New York and London: Harper & Brothers Publishers, 1928) Vol. 2, pp. 635-636.
2. *The War of the Rebellion: A Compilation of the Official Records of the Union and Confederate Armies* (Washington, D.C.: 1880-1901) Series I, Vol. XII, pt. 3, p. 3. (Hereafter cited as O.R.)
3. Ibid., p. 9.
4. Ibid., p. 827.
5. Ibid.
6. Ibid.
7. Ibid., p. 828-829.
8. Ibid., p. 829.
9. Ibid., p. 828.
10. Ibid., p. 834.
11. Rev. William T. Price Papers, H. L. Sheets Collection, Marlinton, W.Va. (Hereafter cited as Price Papers.)
12. Letters of Captain Shephard Green Pryor, Company A, 12th Georgia Infantry, C.S.A. Georgia Department of Archives and History, Atlanta, Ga. (Hereafter cited as Pryor Letters.)
13. Edward Willis Papers, H. E. Huntington Library, San Marion, Calif. (Hereafter cited as Willis Papers.)
14. Pryor Letters.
15. Ibid.
16. Colonel G. F. R. Henderson, *Stonewall Jackson and the American Civil War* (London, New York, Bombay and Calcutta: Longmans, Green, and Co., 1918) Vol. I, p. 265. (Hereafter cited as Henderson.)
17. O.R., Vol. 51, pt. 2, p. 566.
18. Frank S. Reader, *History of the Fifth West Virginia Cavalry, Formerly the Second Virginia Infantry* (New Brighton, Pa.: Daily News, Frank S. Reader, Ed. and Prop., 1890), p. 161. (Hereafter cited as Reader.)
19. Record of Event's Column, Muster Rolls of Company I, 14th Virginia Cavalry. Record Group 109, National Archives, Washington, D.C.
20. Pryor Letters.
21. Reader, p. 161.
22. O.R., Vol. 12, pt. 3, pp. 52-53.
23. Pryor Letters.
24. Reader, p. 161.
25. O.R., Vol. 12, pt. 3, pp. 57-58.
26. Margaret B. Paulus, Comp., *Papers of General Robert Huston Milroy: Milroy Family Letters, 1862-1863* (n.p., 1965) Vol. I. In the Library of Congress, Washington, D.C. (Hereafter cited as Milroy Letters.)
27. O.R., Vol. 12, pt. 3, p. 56.

Chapter II

1. Reader, p. 161.
2. Price Papers.
3. Ibid.

4. Milroy Letters.
5. O.R., Vol. 12, pt. 3, p. 63.
6. Ibid.
7. Reader, p. 161.
8. Price Papers.
9. Reader, p. 162.
10. Price Papers.
11. O.R., Vol. 12, pt. 3, pp. 68-69.
12. Price Papers.
13. Ibid.
14. O.R., Vol. 12, pt. 3, p. 72.
15. Reader, p. 162.
16. Whitelaw Reid. *Ohio In The War: Her Statesman, Her Generals, and Soldiers.* (Cincinnati: Moore, Wilstach & Baldwin, 1868), Vol. 2, pg. 901.
17. Price Papers.
18. Milroy Letters.
19. O.R., Vol. 12, pt. 3, p. 72.
20. Milroy Letters.
21. Reader, pp. 162-163.

Chapter III

1. O.R., Vol. 12, pt. 3, pp. 77-78.
2. Willis Papers.
3. Reader, p. 163.
4. Willis Papers.
5. Ibid.
6. Pryor Letters; S. L. Williams Letters, Virginia Historical Society, Richmond, Va. (Hereafter cited as Williams Letters.)
7. Price Papers.
8. Ibid.; Archie P. McDonald, Ed., *Make Me a Map Of the Valley* (Dallas: Southern Methodist University Press, 1973), p. 43. (Hereafter cited as McDonald.)
9. Willis Papers.
10. O.R., Vol. 12, pt. 3, p. 89.
11. Ibid.
12. Ibid., pp. 90-91.
13. Williams Letters.
14. Milroy Letters.
15. Price Papers.
16. O.R., Vol., 12, pt. 3, pp. 92-93.
17. Ibid., pp. 95-96.
18. McDonald, p. 28.
19. O.R., Vol. 12, pt. 3, p. 852.
20. Robert G. Tanner, *Stonewall In The Valley* (Garden City, New York: Doubleday & Company, Inc., 1976), pp. 145-146. (Hereafter cited as Tanner.)
21. O.R., Vol. 12, pt. 3, p. 852.
22. Ibid., pp. 853-854.
23. McDonald, p. 28.

24. Williams Letters.
25. John M. Ashcraft, Jr., *31st Virginia Infantry,* Lynchburg, Va.: H. E. Howard, Inc., 1988), p. 27. (Hereafter cited as Ashcraft.)
26. Price Papers.
27. Williams Letters.
28. Joseph A. Waddell, *Annals of Augusta County, Virginia* (1902; rpt. Bridgewater, Va.: C. J. Carrier, 1958), p. 469.
29. Pryor Letters.
30. Price Papers.
31. Frank Moore, Ed., *The Rebellion Record: A Diary of American Events, with Documents, Narratives, Illustrative Incidents, Poetry, Etc.,* (New York: G. P. Putnam, 1863), Vol. 5, p. 38. (Hereafter cited as Rebellion Record.)
32. Milroy Letters.
33. McDonald, p. 29.
34. O.R., Vol. 12, pt. 1, pg. 487.
35. O.R., Vol. 12, pt. 3, p. 96.
36. Ibid., Vol. 12, pt. 1, p. 7.
37. Ibid.
38. Ibid., Vol. 12, pt. 3, pg. 104.

Chapter IV

1. O.R., Vol. 51, pt. 2, p. 581.
2. Ibid., Vol. 12, pt. 3, pp. 107-108.
3. Ibid., pp. 99-100.
4. Ibid., p. 105.
5. Price Papers.
6. Reminiscences of Isaac C. Nelson, 73rd Ohio Infantry, in possession of Allan P. Nelson, Skokie, Ill. (Hereafter cited as Nelson.)
7. Diary of John F. Sosman, 73rd Ohio Infantry, George Sosman Family Papers, Western Reserve Historical Society, Cleveland, Ohio. (Hereafter cited as Sosman Diary.)
8. Reader, 163: Richard L. Armstrong, *Ambush At Williamsville, Va.* (Staunton, Va.: The Minute Man Press, 1986), p. 6 (Hereafter cited as Armstrong.)
9. U.S. Pension Record for Thomas J. Walker, 2nd (West) Virginia Infantry, Record Group 94, National Archives, Washington, D.C.
10. Armstrong, p. 7.
11. Price Papers.
12. Willis Papers.
13. O.R., Vol. 12, pt. 3, p. 106.
14. Ibid., pp. 107-108.
15. Reader, p. 163.
16. O.R., Vol. 12, pt. 3, p. 119.
17. Regimental Journal, 73rd Ohio Volunteer Infantry, Record Group 94, National Archives, Washington, D.C. (Hereafter cited as Journal.)
18. Ibid.
19. Ibid.
20. Ibid.
21. Ibid.

22. O.R., Vol. 12, pt. 3, p. 111.
23. Ibid., p. 872.
24. McDonald, p. 34.
25. O.R., Vol. 12, pt. 3, p. 118.
26. Diary of Joseph Snider, 31st Virginia Infantry, in possession of John M. Ash-craft, Jr., Emmaus, Pa. (Hereafter cited as Snider Diary.)
27. Colonel William Couper, *One Hundred Years at V.M.I.,* (Richmond, Va.: Garrett and Massie, Inc., 1939), Vol. 2, p. 146. (Hereafter cited as Couper.)
28. Ibid., p. 147.
29. O.R., Vol. 12, pt. 3, p. 123.
30. Ibid.

Chapter V

1. O.R., Vol. 12, pt. 3, p. 127.
2. Francis F. Wayland, Ed., "Fremont's Pursuit of Jackson in the Shenandoah Valley." *Virginia Magazine of History and Biography,* Vol. 70, (April, July 1962), 167.
3. O.R., Vol. 12, pt. 3, p. 126.
4. Milroy Letters.
5. Frederick, H. Dyer, *A Compendium Of The War Of The Rebellion,* (Dayton, O.: The Press of Morningside Bookshop, 1979), Vol. 1, p. 338.
6. Couper, pp. 195-196.
7. O.R., Vol. 12, pt. 3, p. 879.
8. Reminiscences of John Jehu Trainer, 25th Virginia Infantry, Pocahontas Times, Marlinton, W.Va.
9. Couper, p. 151.
10. Ibid., p. 152.
11. Ibid., p. 153.
12. Ibid., p. 154.
13. McDonald, p. 37.
14. Ibid; Tanner, pp. 165-166.
15. Price Papers.
16. Ibid.
17. Ibid.
18. Ibid.
19. Ibid.
20. Ibid.
21. Letters of J. Q. Barnes, 73rd Ohio Infantry, in the possession of Allan P. Nelson, Skokie, Ill.
22. Ibid.
23. Ibid.
24. Ibid.
25. O.R., Vol. 12, pt. 3, p. 137.
26. Rebellion Record, Vol. 5, p. 38.
27. Thomas M. Rankin, *23rd Virginia Infantry,* (Lynchburg, Va.: H. E. Howard, Inc., 1985), p. 31.
28. Price Papers.
29. Ibid.

Chapter VI

1. O.R., Vol. 12, pt. 3, p. 140.
2. U.S. Pension File, Thomas J. Walker, 2nd (West) Virginia Infantry, Record Group 94, National Archives, Washington, D.C.
3. Ibid.
4. Papers of Jed Hotchkiss, Library of Congress, Washington, D.C. (Hereafter cited as Hotchkiss Papers.)
5. O.R., Vol. 12, pt. 3, p. 879.
6. Joseph A. Waddell, *Annals of Augusta County, Virginia* (1902; rpt. Bridgewater, Va.: C. J. Carrier, 1958), p. 470.
7. R. A. Brock, Ed., *Southern Historical Society Papers* (Richmond, Va., 1920), Vol. 43, p. 183.
8. Charles C. Wright Recollections, Virginia Historical Society, Richmond, Va. (Hereafter cited as Wight Recollections.)
9. E. Z. Hays, *History of the Thirty-Second Regiment Ohio Veteran Volunteer Infantry,* Columbus, O.: Cott & Evans, 1896) p. 23. (Hereafter cited as Hays.)
10. Ibid.
11. Snider Diary; Letters of John F. Sosman, George Sosman Family Papers, Western Reserve Historical Society, Cleveland, O.; Reader, p. 164.
12. Diary of Alexander A. Campbell, 73rd Ohio Infantry, Ohio Historical Society, Columbus, O. (Hereafter cited as Campbell Diary).
13. Hays, p. 24.
14. Hotchkiss Papers.
15. Hays, p. 24.
16. Milroy Letters.
17. Rebellion Record, Vol. 5, p. 38.
18. Recollections of William H. Hull, 31st Virginia Infantry, Pocahontas Times, Marlinton, W.Va. (Hereafter cited as Hull Recollections.)
19. Campbell Diary.
20. Hull Recollections.
21. H. M. Calhoun, *'Twixt North and South,* (Franklin, W.Va.: McCoy Publishing Co., 1974), p. 44.
22. McDonald, p. 38.
23. John Craft Taylor, *Civil War In and About Pendleton County,* (West Virginia, (Thesis, Pennsylvania State University, March 1975), p. 98. (Hereafter cited as Taylor.)
24. Ibid., p. 99.
25. Ibid.
26. O.R., Vol. 12, pt. 3, p. 141.
27. Ibid.
28. Ibid.
29. E. R. Monfort, *From Grafton to McDowell Through Tygart's Valley,* (Cincinnati, O.: H. C. Sherick & Co., 1886), p. 12. (Hereafter cited as Monfort.)
30. Sosman Diary.

Chapter VII

1. Diary of Osborn Wilson, Pocahontas Times, Marlinton, W.Va. (Hereafter cited as Wilson Diary.)

2. Snider Diary.
3. Hotchkiss Papers.
4. Snider Diary; Robert J. Driver, Jr. *52nd Virginia Infantry,* Lynchburg, Va.: H. E. Howard, Inc., 1986.) p. 12. (Hereafter cited as 52nd Virginia Infantry.)
5. Recollections of William H. Hull, Pocahontas Times, Marlinton, W.Va. (Hereafter cited as Hull Recollections.)
6. Reader, p. 164.
7. U.S. War Department. *Atlas To Accompany The Official Records of the Union and Confederate Armies,* (Washington: Government Printing Office, 1891-1895). plate 116, no 1. (Hereafter cited as Atlas.)
8. Frederick H. Dyer, *A Compendium Of The War Of The Rebellion,* (Dayton, O.: The Press of Morningside Bookshop, 1979), Vol. 1, p. 338.
9. O.R., Vol. 12, p. 3, p. 147.
10. Frank Akers and John Scott, *The Battle of McDowell, May 8, 1862: A Terrain Study and Tour,* (n.p.,n.d.) (Hereafter cited as Akers/Scott.)
11. O.R., Vol., 12, p. 1, p. 463.
12. George Weimer Goldthorpe, "The Battle of McDowell, May 8, 1862." *West Virginia History,* Vol. 13, (April, 1952), pp. 183-184. (Hereafter cited as Goldthorpe.)
13. Tanner, p. 171.
14. Reader, p. 164.
15. O.R., Vol. 12, pt. 1, p. 471.
16. Wight Recollections.
17. Atlas, plate 116, No. 1.
18. Cadet File, George H. Smith, V.M.I. Archives, Lexington, Va. (Hereafter cited as Smith, Cadet File.); O.R., Vol. 12, pt. 1, p. 471.; H. M. Calhoun, *'Twixt North and South,* (Franklin, W.Va.: McCoy Publishing Company, 1974), p. 42. (Hereafter cited as Calhoun.)
19. Wilson Diary; Robert J. Driver, Jr., *1st and 2nd Rockbridge Artillery,* (Lynchburg, Va.: H. E. Howard, Inc., 1987), p. 19.
20. John S. Robson, How a One-Legged Rebel Lives, (Gaithersburg, Maryland: Butternut Press, 1984), p. 29.
21. O.R., Vol. 12, pt. 3, pp. 147-148.
22. Ibid.
23. Hartwell Osborn, *Trials and Triumphs: The Record of the Fifty-Fifth Ohio Volunteer Infantry,* (Chicago: A. C. McClurg, 1904), p. 26.
24. Akers/Scott.
25. Hotchkiss Papers.
26. O.R., Vol. 12, pt. 1, p. 468.

Chapter VIII

1. Monfort, p. 14.
2. John D. Imboden, "Stonewall Jackson In The Shenandoah Valley," *Battles and Leaders of the Civil War,* (New York: Thomas Yoseloff, 1956), p. 298. (Hereafter cited as Imboden.)
3. Ibid.
4. Hays, p. 24.
5. Kevin C. Ruffner, *44th Virginia Infantry,* (Lynchburg, Va.: H. E. Howard, Inc.,

1987), p. 24. (Hereafter cited as Ruffner.)

6. Ibid.
7. Goldthorpe, p. 186.
8. Rebellion Record, p. 38.
9. O.R., Vol. 12, p. 1, pp. 468-469.
10. Robert L. Dabney, *Life and Campaigns of Lieutenant General Thomas J. Jackson,* (New York: Bielock and Co., 1866), pp. 348-349.
11. Goldthorpe, pp. 201-202.
12. O.R., Vol. 12, pt. 1, p. 486.
13. Ibid.
14. Goldthorpe, pp. 190-191.
15. O.R., Vol. 12, pt. 1, p. 469.
16. Rebellion Record, p. 39.
17. Samuel H. Hurst, *Journal-History of the Seventy-Third Ohio Volunteer Infantry,* (Chillicothe: 1866), p. 18. (Hereafter cited as Hurst.)
18. Alfred E. Lee, "Our First Battle: Bull Pasture Mountain." *Magazine of American History,* Martha J. Lamb, ed. (New York City:) Vol. 15 (Jan.-June 1886), 391-396. (Hereafter cited as Lee Article.)
19. Lee Article.
20. O.R., Vol. 12, pt. 1, p. 466.
21. Milroy Letters.
22. Reader, p. 165.
23. Ephraim Hutchison, "McDowell: Our Little Band of Heroes." *Civil War Times Illustrated,* David C. Cornelius, ed. (Harrisburg, Pa.: Historical Times, Inc.) Vol. 21, No. 5 (Sept. 1982), p. 39. (Hereafter cited as Hutchison Letter.)
24. Andrew Price, "West Virginia Anthology, The Battle of McDowell and Some Lights on the Life and Character of General Milroy." *West Virginia Blue Book,* (Charleston: 1926), Vol. 11, p. 444. (Hereafter cited as Price, Blue Book.)
25. Theodore F. Lang, *Loyal West Virginia from 1861 to 1865.* (Baltimore: Deutsch Pub. Co., 1895), pp. 220-221.
26. Rebellion Record, p. 39.
27. Goldthorpe, p. 194.
28. O.R., Vol. 12, pt. 1, p. 477.
29. Wilson Diary.
30. Smith, Cadet File.
31. Goldthorpe, p. 192.
32. Monfort, pp. 17-18.
33. 52nd Virginia Infantry, p. 196.

Chapter IX

1. *The Highland Recorder,* (Monterey, Va.) "The Battle of McDowell", Recollections of George W. Sponaugle. Feb. 25, 1927. (Hereafter cited as Sponaugle Account.)
2. Hutchison Letter.
3. Thomas M. Rankin, *37th Virginia Infantry,* (Lynchburg, Va.: H. E. Howard, Inc., 1987), p. 32. (Hereafter cited as 37th Virginia Infantry.)
4. Thomas M. Rankin, *23rd Virginia Infantry,* (Lynchburg, Va.: H. E. Howard, 1985), p. 32.

5. 37th Virginia Infantry, p. 32.
6. *The Daily News Record,* (Harrisonburg), 2/6/1914, "Dashing Confederate Veteran. . ." (Hereafter cited as Daily News Record.); *The Highland Recorder,* (Monterey, Va.), 5/20/98, "The McDowell Reunion." (Hereafter cited as Reunion Article.)
7. Reunion Article.
8. Ruffner, p. 24.
9. O.R., Vol. 12, pt. 1, p. 486.
10. John Chapla, *42nd Virginia Infantry,* (Lynchburg, Va.: H. E. Howard, Inc., 1983), p. 13. (Hereafter cited as 42nd Virginia Infantry.)
11. O.R., Vol. 12, pt. 1, p. 480.
12. Ibid., p. 479.
13. Ibid.
14. John Chapla, *48th Virginia Infantry,* (Lynchburg, Va.: H. E. Howard, Inc., 1989), p. 22. (Hereafter citied as 48th Virginia Infantry.)
15. Ibid.
16. Ibid., p. 126.
17. Memoirs of Martin W. Brett, Company F, 12th Georgia Infantry. Emory University, The Robert W. Woodruff Library, Atlanta, Ga.
18. Hotchkiss Papers.
19. Ibid.
20. Ibid.
21. Ibid.
22. O.R., Vol. 12, pt. 1, p. 467.
23. Ibid., p. 464.
24. Reader, p. 165.
25. Milroy Letters.
26. Sosman Diary.
27. Report of Colonel James Cantwell, 82nd Ohio Infantry, Union Battle Reports, RG-94, Box 21, Vol. 12. National Archives, Washington, D.C.
28. Hutchison Letter.
29. Ibid.
30. Goldthorpe, p. 201.
31. Snider Diary.
32. Hotchkiss Papers.
33. Snider Diary.

Chapter X

1. Tanner, p. 173; An account left by one of the Cadets, B. A. Colonna, does not make any mention of this detail on the night of the 8th. Jennings C. Wise, *The Military History of the Virginia Military Institute from 1839 to 1865,* (Lynchbyurg, Va.: J. P. Bell Company, Inc., 1915), pp. 206-207. (Hereafter cited as Wise.)
2. Wight Recollections.
3. O.R., Vol. 12, pt. 1, p. 461; Milroy Letters; Hutchison Letter.
4. O.R., Vol. 12, pt. 1, pp. 28-29.
5. Hurst, p. 19.
6. McDonald, p. 43.

7. Snider Diary.
8. Imboden, pp. 287-288.
9. Oren F. Morton, *A History of Highland County Virginia,* (Baltimore: Regional Publishing Co., 1969), p. 130.
10. Sponaugle Account.
11. Lowell Reidenbaugh, *33rd Virginia Infantry,* (Lynchburg, Va.: H. E. Howard, Inc., 1987), p. 28.
12. Wise, pp. 207-208.
13. Goldthorpe, p. 205.
14. Alexander Caldwell Jones Papers, Virginia Historical Society, Richmond, Va.
15. O.R., Vol. 12, pt. 1, p. 491.
16. *The Highland Recorder,* (Monterey, Va.), no date, "From the Recollections of the Late H. H. Seybert: Highland In the Civl War." (Hereafter cited as Seybert Recollections).
17. O.R., Vol. 12, pt. 3, p. 157.
18. Goldthorpe, p. 204.
19. Wilson Diary.
20. Hotchkiss Papers.
21. Goldthorpe, p. 206.
22. McDonald, p. 43.
23. Harry Gilmor, *Four Years in the Saddle,* New York: Harper, 1866), pp. 36-37. (Hereafter cited as Gilmor.)
24. O.R., Vol. 12, pt. 3, p. 172.
25. Ibid.
26. Ibid., p. 173.
27. Taylor, p. 95.
28. Sponaugle Account.
29. Ibid.
30. O.R., Vol. 12, pt. 3, p. 888.
31. Gilmor, pp. 38-39.
32. Tanner, p. 179.
33. Ibid.
34. O.R., Vol. 12, pt. 3, p. 889.
35. George Hay Stuart Papers, Letter of J. K. Boswell, Library of Congress, Washington, D.C.

Chapter XI
1. McDonald, p. 45.
2. Compiled Service Records of Confederate Generals and Staff Officers, and Nonregimental Enlisted Men, File of Edward Johnson. RG-109, M-331, National Archives, Washington, D.C.
3. Snider Diary.
4. Tanner, p. 180.
5. Hull Recollections.
6. Tanner, p. 195.

BIBLIOGRAPHY

Manuscripts

Akers, Frank and Scott, John. *The Battle of McDowell, May 8, 1862: A Terrain Study and Tour.* no date, unpublished.
Ashcraft, John M. Jr., Emmaus, Pa.
    Notes concerning the battle of McDowell
    Diary of Joseph Snider
Deitz, Mrs. T. O., Covington, Va.
    Diary of James McClintic
Durant, Don, Zanesville, Ohio.
    "The Battle of McDowell", unpublished poem
Emory University, The Robert W. Woodruff Library, Atlanta, Ga.
    Memoir of Martin W. Brett
Georgia Department of Archives and History, Atlanta, Ga.
    Shepherd Green Pryor Letters
Henry E. Huntington Library and Art Gallery, San Marino, Calif.
    Edward Willis Papers
Krick, Robert K., Fredericksburg, Va.
    Notes concerning the Battle of McDowell
Library of Congress, Washington, D.C.
    Papers of Jedediah Hotchkiss
    Papers of Robert H. Milroy
    George Hay Stuart Papers, Letter of J. K. Boswell
National Archives, Washington, D.C.
    Compiled Military Service Records of Confederate Generals and Staff Officers, and Nonregimental Enlisted Men. M - 331.
    Union Battle Reports, RG - 94, Box 21, Vol. 12.
Ohio Historical Society, Columbus, O.
    Diary of Thomas Evans
    Alexander A. Campbell Papers
Sheets, Harry L., Marlinton, W.Va.
    William T. Price Papers
Virginia Historical Society, Richmond, Va.
    S. L. Williams Papers
    Alexander Caldwell Jones Papers
    Recollections of Charles C. Wight
Watkins, Raymond. Falls Church, Va.
    Notes concerning the battle of McDowell
    List of Deaths at the battle of McDowell

Western Reserve Historical Society, Cleveland, O.
   Letters and Diary of John F. Sosman, George Sosman Family Papers

Published Works

Allan, William. *Stonewall Jackson's Campaign in the Shenandoah Valley of Virginia.* London: Hugh Rees, Ltd., 1912.

Ashcraft, John M. Jr. *31st Virginia Infantry.* Lynchburg, Va.: H. E. Howard, Inc., 1988.

Calhoun, H. M. *'Twixt North and South.* Franklin W.Va.: McCoy Publishing Company, 1974

Chapla, John D. *42nd Virginia Infantry.* Lynchburg, Va.: H. E. Howard, Inc., 1983.

Chapla, John D. *48th Virginia Infantry.* Lynchburg, Va.: H. E. Howard, Inc., 1989.

Cooke, John Esten. *The Life of Stonewall Jackson.* New York: Charles B. Richardson, 1866.

Couper, Colonel William. *One Hundred Years at V.M.I.* Richmond, Virginia: Garrett and Massie, Inc., 4 Volumes, 1939.

Dabney, R. L. *Life and Campaigns of Lieut.-General Thomas J. Jackson.* New York: Blelock & Co., 1866.

Driver, Robert J., Jr. *The 1st and 2nd Rockbridge Artillery.* Lynchburg, Va.: H. E. Howard, Inc., 1987.

Driver, Robert J. Jr. *52nd Virginia Infantry.* Lynchburg, Va.: H. E. Howard, Inc., 1986.

Dyer, Frederick Henry. *A Compendium of the War of the Rebellion.* Dayton, O.: The Press of Morningside Bookshop, 1979.

Gilmor, Harry. Four Years in the Saddle. New York: Harper & Brothers, 1866.

Goldthorpe, George Weimer. "The Battle of McDowell, May 8, 1862. *West Virginia History.* Charleston, W.Va.: State Department of Archives and History, Vol. 13, No. 3 (April, 1952).

Hall, James E. *Diary of A Confederate Soldier.* Philippi, W.Va.: Elizabeth Teter Philips, 1961.

Hays, E. Z., Ed. *History of the Thirty-Second Regiment Ohio Veteran Volunteer Infantry.* Columbus, Ohio: Cott & Evans, Printers, 1896.

Henderson, Colonel G. F. R. *Stonewall Jackson and the American Civil War.* London: Longmans, Green, and Co., 1913.

Howard, McHenry. *Recollections of a Maryland Confederate Soldier and Staff Officer Under Johnston, Jackson and Lee.* Baltimore: Williams & Wilkins Company, 1914.

Hurst, Samuel H. *Journal-History of the Seventy-Third Ohio Volunteer Infantry.* Chillicothe, Ohio: 1866.

Hutchison, Ephriam. "McDowell: Our Little Band of Heroes" ed. David. C. Cornelius. *Civil War Times Illustrated,* Harrisburg, Pa. Vol. 21, No. 5 (Sept. 1982).

Imboden, John D. "Stonewall Jackson in the Shenandoah." *Battles and Leaders of the Civil War.* New York: Thomas Yoseloff Inc., Vol. 2, 1956.

Lang, Theodore F. *Loyal West Virginia from 1861 to 1865.* Baltimore: Deutsch Pub. Co., 1895.

Lee, Alfred E. "Our First Battle: Bull Pasture Mountain." *Magazine of American History,* ed. Martha J. Lamb. New York, New York: Vol. 15, Jan.-June, 1886.

McDonald, Archie P., Ed. *Make Me a Map Of the Valley: The Civil War Journal of Stonewall Jackson's Topographer.* Dallas: Southern Methodist University Press, 1973.

Manarin, Louis H. and Wallace, Lee A. Jr. *Richmond Volunteers, 1861-1865: The Volunteer Companies of the City of Richmond and Henrico County, Virginia.* Richmond: Westover Press, 1969.

Moore, Frank, Ed. *The Rebellion Record: A Diary of American Events.* New York: G. P. Putnam, 12 Volumes, 1852-7.

Monfort, E. R. *From Grafton to McDowell, Through Tygart's Valley.* Cincinnati: H. C. Sherick & Co., 1886.

Morton, Oren F. *A History of Highland County, Virginia.* Baltimore: Regional Publishing Company, 1969.

Morton, Oren F. *A Handbook of Highland County and A supplement to Pendleton and Highland History.* Monterey, Va.: The Highland Recorder, 1922.

Murphy, Terrence V. *10th Virginia Infantry.* Lynchburg, Va.: H. E. Howard, Inc., 1989.

Osborn, Captain Hartwell. *Trials And Triumphs: The Record of the Fifty-fifth Ohio Volunteer Infantry.* Chicago: A. C. McClurg & Co., 1904.

Price, Andrew. "West Virginia Anthology: The Battle of McDowell and Some Lights on the Life and Character of General Milroy." *West Virginia Blue Book.* No publisher or date, Vol. 11. (1926).

Rankin, Thomas M. *23rd Virginia Infantry.* Lynchburg, Va.: H. E. Howard, Inc., 1985.

Rankin, Thomas M. *37th Virginia Infantry.* Lynchburg, Va.: H. E. Howard, Inc., 1987.

Reader, Frank Smith. *History of the Fifth West Virginia Cavalry, Formerly the 2nd Virginia Infantry and of Battery G, First West Va. Light Artillery.* New Brighton, Pa., Daily News, Frank S. Reader, Editor and Prop., 1890.

Reid, Whitelaw. *Ohio In The War: Her Statesman, Her Generals, and Soldiers.* Cincinnati: Moore, Wilstach & Baldwin, Vol. 2. 1868.

Reidenbaugh, Lowell. *33rd Virginia Infantry.* Lynchburg, Va.: H. E. Howard, Inc., 1987.

Ruffner, Kevin C. *44th Virginia Infantry.* Lynchburg, Va.: H. E. Howard, Inc., 1987.

Scott, W. W., Ed. "Diary of a Capt. H. W. Wingfield." *Bulletin of the Virginia State Library.* Richmond: Davis Bottom, Superintendent of Public Printing, 1927.

Tanner, Robert G. *Stonewall In The Valley.* Garden City, New York: Doubleday & Company, Inc., 1976.

Taylor, John Craft. *Civil War In and About Pendleton County, (West) Virginia.* Unpublished Thesis, The Pennsylvania State University, March 1975.

U.S. War Department. *War of the Rebellion: A Compilation of the official Records of the Union and Confederate Armies.* 128 Volumes. Washington, D.C.: U.S. Government Printing Office, 1880-1901.

Waddell, Joseph A. *Annals of Augusta Co., Va.* Bridgewater, Va.: C. J. Carrier, Co., 1958.

Wallace, Lee A. Jr. *A Guide To Virginia Military Organizations, 1861-1865.* Lynchburg, Va.: H. E. Howard, Inc., 1986.

Wayland, Francis F. "Fremont's Pursuit of Jackson in the Shenandoah Valley", *The Virginia Magazine of History and Biography,* Richmond: Virginia Historical Society. Vol. 70, No. 2 (April 1962)

Wise, Jennings C. *The Military History Of The Virginia Military Institute From 1839 to 1865.* Lynchburg, Va.: J. P. Bell Company, Inc., 1915.

Worsham, John H. *One of Jackson's Foot Cavalry.* New York: Neale Publishing Co., 1912.

Newspapers

Daily News-Record, Harrisonburg, Va.
Daily Virginian, Lynchburg, Va.
The Highland Recorder, Monterey, Va.
The Pocahontas Times, Marlinton, W.Va.

Periodicals

Southern Historical Society Papers. Richmond, 1876-1953. 52 Volumes.

INDEX